EASY
ORCHIDS

EASY
ORCHIDS

LIZ JOHNSON

FIREFLY BOOKS

FIREFLY BOOKS

Published by Firefly Books Ltd. 2005
Copyright © 2005 Collins & Brown
Copyright text © Liz Johnson

First printing
Publisher Cataloging-in-Publication
Data (U.S.)

Johnson, Liz.
    Easy orchids : the fail-safe guide to
growing orchids indoors / Liz
Johnson. —1st ed.
[144] p. : col. photos. ;   cm.
Includes index.
Summary: Includes advice and tips on
how to choose a suitable orchid for
your home, techniques for care and
cultivation and a directory of 85
orchids that are easy to grow inside.
ISBN 1-55297-935-0
ISBN 1-55297-938-5   (pbk.)
1. Orchid culture. 2. Orchid culture --
Handbooks, manuals, etc. 3. Orchids -
- Varieties. I. Title.
635.9/3415 22   SB409.A3J64 2005

Library and Archives Canada
Cataloguing in Publication

Johnson, Liz (Liz I.)
        Easy orchids : the fail-safe
guide to growing orchids indoors / Liz
Johnson.

ISBN 1-55297-935-0 (bound).--ISBN 1-
55297-938-5 (pbk.)

        1. Orchid culture. 2.
Orchids. 3. Indoor gardening. I. Title.

SB409.J63 2005   635.9'344 C2004-
905607-7

Published in the United States by
Firefly Books (U.S.) Inc.
P.O. Box 1338, Ellicott Station
Buffalo, New York 14205
Published in Canada by
Firefly Books Ltd.
66 Leek Crescent
Richmond Hill, Ontario L4B 1H1
Printed by Imago, Singapore

CONTENTS

Introduction

THERE ARE ORCHID BOOKS for academics, amateur collectors, and enthusiasts, but none for those who love and buy orchids purely as plants to decorate their homes and gardens. This book aims to provide a practical, concise, easy-to-use guide that is suitable for those with little or no experience of growing orchids.

Orchids have long been considered expensive and difficult to grow, and the myth that has built up around these fabulous plants needs dispelling. There is a wide choice of easy-to-grow orchids that will happily live in most homes.

Many people may have come across a stunning orchid, but were discouraged by the uninformative plant label. It is not unusual for the instructions on such labels to be so general that they are virtually useless. In this book I will explain the basic rules for selecting your orchid, caring for it properly and getting it to reflower. Once you know the basic techniques, you will get enormous enjoyment and satisfaction from growing these wonderful plants.

Below: A *Cymbidium* is a good choice for beginners to grow in cool conditions.

Right: *Phalaenopsis* have long-lasting flowers and make an excellent plant for your home.

Central heating and other modern heating systems have resulted in a dramatic rise in the popularity of the moth orchid as a houseplant. Discovered in the jungles of the Philippines, it has elegant, arching sprays of flowers that shimmer in the breeze like fluttering, fragile moths. *Phalaenopsis* now tops plant popularity polls in the U.S., the U.K. and other parts of Europe.

The past two years saw the moth orchid share top spot as the U.K.'s most popular pot plant, and it has achieved the number two position in the U.S., just behind the ever-popular Christmas poinsettia. The pages of lifestyle and decorating magazines and television shows bring us images, week after week, of orchids used as decorative features in the home. Their use is understandable: they are truly beautiful and available in a range of colors, shapes and sizes. Many are easy to grow and do not require constant attention.

As for my own orchid "credentials"—I am the owner of McBean's Orchids in Cooksbridge, in southeast England, a company that has grown orchids since 1879. Over a century of breeding and showing these amazing plants has gained McBean's nursery countless awards and worldwide recognition. I have written this book with the orchid as a houseplant firmly in mind. I'm backed by a wealth of experience from the team at McBean's, who have bred and raised several million orchids.

Chapter 1

CHOOSING
YOUR ORCHID

Buying an orchid for the home should be a pleasurable experience. Where should you start? Many people receive their first orchid as a gift or they make an impulse buy when shopping. In most cases these orchids will be among the "easy-to-grow" varieties, but taking a little time to choose the right orchid plant can bring rewards. Those who claim that all orchids are difficult to grow have probably had a bad experience. Perhaps their plant was totally unsuited to their lifestyle, or they didn't have the right information about how to care for it, or maybe the plant was not healthy when it was purchased. It takes only a little time to choose a healthy plant that will thrive in your home environment, and it will be time well spent.

The right orchid for your home

THE ESSENTIAL THING TO REMEMBER is that different types of orchids need different growing conditions. In this book, I will explain how to check that your intended purchase is right for your home and the position where you will place it. Generally, orchids are divided into three groups: warm-growing, intermediate-growing and cool-growing.

It makes sense that a warm-growing plant will not survive in an unheated, drafty porch, or that a cool-growing one will die from heat exhaustion if placed near a radiator in a warm room. Unfortunately, the sales staff in some outlets have little knowledge of the plants they sell and are unlikely to be able to give you good advice about what to choose. The colored plant labels accompanying orchids often don't give much information, and what there is may be under a general heading of "orchid," which is not particularly useful. Advice is more readily available from specialist nurseries. Arming yourself with a little knowledge from this book will give you the confidence to make a suitable choice.

Popular choices

Orchids vary tremendously in size, shape and color. There are thought to be more than 30,000 species growing naturally in the wild all over the world. Then there are literally millions of hybrids, the vast majority of which are produced by nurseries. Not all are suitable as houseplants, but the number that are is increasing annually.

Below: *Phalaenopsis* Brother Little Amaglad is a popular choice. It's not too tall and has dainty, soft pink flowers.

Moth orchid (*Phalaenopsis*)

There are thousands of different varieties of moth orchid, *Phalaenopsis*. They may produce sprays of large, round flowers in white, pink or yellow. They can also be found with spots or stripes, with contrasting colored centers or edges. Some moth orchids may have masses of tiny flowers or, more unusually, a few flowers in stunning reds or glowing golds. In fact, because the moth orchid has been discovered to be an ideal houseplant, growers have concentrated their efforts on producing a huge selection of this particular orchid. The downside is that it has become harder to find the same named varieties year after year. The moth orchid has become a fashion item and growers are looking for something new each year, both in color and style.

Cymbidium

The *Cymbidium* has long been popular as a houseplant in the U.K. and as a corsage orchid in the U.S. Unlike the moth orchid, it is not happy growing inside all year round. Many originated in the foothills of the Himalayas and prefer a cooler existence, particularly at night. Before the advent of central heating, the *Cymbidium* was happy to grow in most places inside during the frosty winter months, which is its flowering period. Today, it may be difficult to find a cool spot in some homes, but not impossible.

Cymbidiums benefit from being placed outdoors in the summer—which is a bonus, as you don't have to find a place in your home for a pot full of dull leaves, while you wait for the next flowering period. The blooms are long-lasting and famous for their range of colors—whites, creams, pinks, reds, yellows, oranges, greens and browns.

These are just two of the groups of orchids that are easy to grow in the home, although the conditions they prefer are quite different. In this book you will find many more. Just check that the plant you would like to buy will grow happily in the place you intend to put it.

Above: *Cymbidium* Highland Hill 'Cooksbridge Rajah' has large, showy flowers and prefers cool growing conditions.

Positioning your orchid

Where will the orchid live in your home? Do you have central heating and keep your house at a daytime temperature above 71°F (22°C)? If so, your best choice may be a plant from the warm-growing orchid group. You may be able to grow plants that prefer lower temperatures, but they will not bloom as well or for as long as they might. If your living room is warm, but the bedrooms are cooler, it means you have two different environments to offer.

If you have a traditionally heated home that relies on coal fires or a wood-burning stove, you will probably have colder areas in the house that are just the right temperature for cooler-growing orchids.

Some homes have a conservatory that is regularly used for dining or relaxing, and this is a popular area for growing orchids. Conservatories can be tricky, though—searing summer temperatures might be fine for tropical plants, but glass will concentrate the heat and destroy an orchid's

Above: Conservatories make popular places for growing orchids, but remember to provide adequate shading and ventilation.

leaf cells unless a degree of shading is used. Most people do not want a shady conservatory! Also, some conservatories are unheated when they are not in use, for example, during the winter. No orchid will be able to survive that sort of extreme fluctuation in temperature, from 95°F (35°C) to as low as 32°F (0°C). However, if you are prepared to move your orchids for the winter and provide some shade and humidity during the summer, they will be able to prosper and look stunning in a conservatory.

Most of us grow plants on a windowsill. Clearly, size will be a consideration when choosing any plant, but the aspect of the window is important, too. Direct sunlight through a south-facing window will cause burning. An east- or west-facing window is preferable. Also bear in mind what will happen if you close blinds or curtains. Will the plant be left in the cold?

Bathrooms are often regarded as good places to grow orchids because of the humid atmosphere and misty glass when we bathe or shower. However, there are some potential drawbacks to consider. Unlike the furnishings of other rooms, the cool walls and floors of bathrooms quickly lose heat. The light levels are often too low, with small windows usually made of frosted glass. Although many orchids prefer shade, the overall light level must be high enough for the plant to make its food.

Most homes will probably have several different types of environments to offer an orchid. If you know where you want to keep your orchid, then look for those plants that will thrive in that situation. If you are given an orchid as a gift, check where it prefers to grow and position it in the most suitable place in your house.

Above: Miniature *Cymbidium* Sarah Jean 'Ice Cascade,' trailing and dainty for a cool spot.

Below: Orchids make good companions for other plants.

Buying from a retail outlet

THERE ARE SEVERAL DIFFERENT TYPES of retail outlets that you can visit to make your selection. These range from large DIY chains, supermarkets, florists and garden centers to specialist orchid nurseries. Orchids are also available by mail order, from catalogs or via the Web.

What to look out for

Having decided which type of orchid you'd like to buy, what else should you look for when faced with a shelf of plants? Appearances will tell you a lot. You are looking for the longest flowering period possible, so check that open flowers are really fresh. Disregard any plants with sad, drooping flowers or petals with browned edges. Any buds should be green and pert.

Look closely at the leaves. Are there signs of pests or disease? Some orchids naturally have yellowish-green leaves, while others have dark green ones, so this can't be used as a guide. Do check, however, that there are no patches of yellow or brown on the leaves. Refuse any plant with shriveled leaves, which is a sign of dehydration or root rot.

Many orchids, particularly moth orchids, are grown in transparent plastic pots. Check that there is a good root system and that the roots are neither dried up (shriveled and flat), nor black and soggy.

Unless you want to buy a hardy orchid, avoid plants that are displayed outside. Being placed outdoors would be a shock to any orchid that has been grown and cared for in a greenhouse. It is also a warning sign that the retailer does not know how to care for them properly.

Having made your purchase, make sure that your orchid is wrapped to protect it from sudden temperature changes. Abrupt fluctuations can cause the buds to drop. When you get home, unwrap the plant immediately and check to see if it needs watering. Then place it in its new home and enjoy it.

CHECKLIST

- Fresh buds and/or fresh flowers
- Free from pests
- Free from disease
- Correct level of hydration
- A healthy root system
- No transit damage
- No signs of poor storage, e.g. leaf damage
- Are you buying from a reputable nursery or retailer?
- Does the seller offer advice?
- Is the orchid right for your lifestyle?

Left: Healthy (far left) and unhealthy root systems of a *Cymbidium* are shown here. As most moth orchids are for sale in transparent pots, it should be easy to check their roots. Retailers would be very unhappy about plants being pulled out of their pots to be examined by potential buyers!

Buying by mail order or via the Internet

WHEN YOU BUY BY MAIL ORDER OR VIA THE INTERNET, there are a few other points to bear in mind. Obviously, you can't inspect the plant before you buy, so it is sensible to choose your source carefully. My recommendation is to seek out a long-established orchid nursery that is experienced in sending out orchids. They will be able to select a suitable plant for you and will ensure that it is properly protected when mailed. They will also know when not to send it. Parcels left overnight at a warehouse in bad weather conditions or extreme heat can cause your plant distress and damage.

With the advent of the Internet, you can go online and find nurseries all over the world, offering the most exotic of plants, often at very reasonable prices. Be warned—buying from overseas is not easy and is actively discouraged. Read the information below.

Regulations and controls

Orchids belong to a list of plants that are classified as endangered. The Washington Convention on International Endangered Species of Wild Fauna and Flora, commonly known as CITES, rigorously controls the sale and movement of all orchids, not just those from the wild, and some are prohibited completely. Currently, to move any orchid from one country to another requires permission and documentation from both the exporting and importing authorities. Another requirement is a health certificate. Each plant has to be inspected before export to ensure that it is free from pests and disease. The charges for CITES and plant health documentation vary, as does the time it takes to acquire it. (Note: these regulations do not apply when moving plants within member countries of the European Union.)

It may be tempting to ignore the rules and regulations, but to do so is unwise. I have known people who, in spite of warnings, have purchased

Below: The majority of hybrid orchids are manmade and not endangered, but they still require CITES documentation if purchased overseas.

plants without documentation, only to have them destroyed on import. As a general rule, it is far better to buy from a local nursery. The orchid may cost a little more, but the nursery will have shouldered the costs of importing it and paid for all the necessary inspections. The nursery will know if the particular orchid you want is a suitable choice for your home. This sort of personal advice can save you a great deal of disappointment and money.

Check sizes

It's a good idea to check the size of the plant on offer and its flower. Close-ups can be deceptive—a tiny flower can fill a screen if a powerful camera has been used. Plants are not always for sale when they are in bud or flower. They can be offered as juvenile plants that may take several years to flower, near flowering size (read carefully what this means in each case), at flowering size (when the plant is expected to flower in the coming season) or mature. Mature plants will have flowered at least once, but might still have a lot of growing to do. Plants "in spike" will have one or more flower stems, and these can be "in bud" or "in flower."

CHECKLIST
- Are you buying from a reputable nursery or retailer?
- Overseas sellers must supply CITES and health documentation (not applicable for purchase between EU member countries)
- Import permits are required for overseas purchases
- Check that plants have not been collected from the wild
- Check the size of the plant on offer. Is it in bud or flower?
- Check the size of the bloom. Close-ups can be deceptive.
- Is overnight delivery possible?
- Does the seller offer advice?
- Is the orchid right for your lifestyle?

Below: Orchids can be purchased as tiny plants in growing flasks up to large, mature plants.

Chapter 2

LOOKING AFTER YOUR ORCHID

Although easy to care for, like most other living things, the orchids included in this book still require adequate light, water, food and a suitable environment in order to thrive. Orchids grown as houseplants will need to suit your lifestyle to bloom well. On the following pages you will find hundreds of varieties of orchids that are no more demanding than many other houseplants.

Keep your orchid happy

Now we will take a look at the basic NEEDS of your orchids and what to do if things go wrong.

Temperature

The myth that all orchids need very hot temperatures and high humidity still exists. Visions of tropical rain forests or an old-fashioned hot house spring to mind. Fortunately, this is not the case—orchids grow all over the world at vastly different temperatures. While some do originate from tropical rain forests, others can be found growing happily in cooler climates like the British marshlands. To grow any orchid successfully depends on providing it with temperatures close to those in its natural habitat.

This is not as difficult as might at first appear. The advent of central heating has given us the opportunity to grow tropical orchids, such as the moth orchid, in our living rooms. Not so long ago, our houses were decorated with plants such as azaleas and aspidistras. These have lost their appeal because they prefer chillier environments and consequently do not last long in warmer houses.

To help select an orchid that is right for your lifestyle, choose from the group that thrive in temperatures nearest to those you like to live in.

Cool: day 64°F (18°C), minimum night 50°F (10°C)
Intermediate: day 68°F (20°C), minimum night 55°F (13°C)
Warm: day 68°F (20°C) or higher, minimum night 60°F (16°C)

These are guidelines only. The most important consideration is the daytime climate. Don't be put off by the night temperatures. Some orchids need only a small drop in temperature at night, while others, such as the *Cymbidium*, like much cooler nights.

Warm-growing orchids can survive the occasional, lower night temperature, but they are certainly not happy below 53°F (12°C). Although it won't die, your plant will not bloom, either. If your conditions are near to these minimums, keep your orchid quite dry. Higher daytime temperatures are no problem with these plants if they have a shady position, good humidity and air circulation.

Light

This is one of the basic requirements for healthy growth and ultimately for flower production. Light can affect the number of flowers produced and their color intensity.

Orchids can be divided roughly into three groups when it comes to light: those that prefer full sun, those that prefer shade, and those that grow best in indirect sunlight. The majority of orchids fall into the last category because most are epiphytes (air plants). In the wild, these orchids attach themselves to a support, usually a tree, with specially produced roots. The orchids benefit from the shade provided, but they are not parasites and do not harm their support.

So what exactly is indirect sunlight in your home? There are ways of measuring light levels, often quoted in "foot-candles." It is not necessary

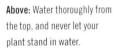

to worry about such precision when growing orchids as houseplants. A far easier guide is to hold your hand about 10 in (25 cm) in front of your plant, between it and the direction of the sun or its light source. If a shadow is produced, the plant is too near the light. Either move it farther away or provide some form of shading such as a sheer curtain or a blind.

The amount of light your orchid needs can change with fluctuations in temperature and humidity. Light intensity changes throughout the year. More shade will be needed in the summer to help maintain suitable temperature and humidity levels.

Water

This is the subject that causes great anxiety and raises the largest number of questions. As I have mentioned, many wild orchids grow attached to a tree for support by aerial roots. Other roots hang loose, absorbing the moisture from the atmosphere. In your home, the orchid will absorb moisture in two ways: from the atmosphere and from the water you give it.

Above: Water thoroughly from the top, and never let your plant stand in water.

Most orchids prefer water that is low in calcium, and in some areas tap water fits this description. However, as a rule, water is treated to make it fit for human consumption by adding chemicals that are too strong for the majority of orchids and could cause root burn. Sensitive orchids, which would not be classed as easy to grow, cannot tolerate tap water at all. Rainwater, however, is usually fine for all orchids. If your access to rainwater is limited, I suggest mixing tap water and rainwater in equal proportions. This will dilute any strong salts in the tap water to an acceptable level. If you don't have any rainwater, use filtered water instead. All water should be at room temperature to prevent shocking your plant. If possible, water in the morning to give any standing water time to evaporate.

How often to water

How often you water depends on many factors: the type of orchid, its age, the temperature it grows at, the type of container or support, the growing medium and its growing season. Check the growing guide for your orchid, which will tell you what to keep in mind. For most of the easy-to-grow orchids, there is one golden rule. When you water, do so thoroughly and allow the plant to drain adequately. Water from the top, taking care to keep the center of the plant dry. Never let your plant stand in excess water, and if the pot is placed inside another container, make sure it isn't standing in trapped water.

The weight of the pot is a good indicator of moisture content, as water is quite heavy. Try weighing the pot in your hand, both when it is dry and just after it has been thoroughly watered. This will help you judge when to water. Remember, the top of the growing medium may be dry, but underneath it could be damp.

Humidity

The orchids included in this book do not require high humidity levels and large amounts of misting. Only orchids grown at high temperatures or mounted on bark, instead of being grown in a pot, will need regular spraying (*see page 24*).

When dealing with orchids that can be grown in the home or the garden, the main concern is to take care that the atmosphere does not become too dry. This can happen in centrally heated homes. The first telltale signs are browning at the tips of the leaves or flower petals. In the case of the moth orchid, the buds drop.

All orchids like a fresh, airy atmosphere and adequate ventilation. If you live in a dry atmosphere, stand the plant on a tray of moist gravel to create a humid microclimate and encourage growth. Make sure that the base of the pot is above the water level. Placing the pot on an upturned saucer would help raise it slightly. Grouping several plants together, or including some ferns on the tray, not only makes an attractive arrangement, but also helps humidity levels. Gently misting the plants early in the morning is useful if the air is very dry. Take care not to do this at low temperatures because small black spots of *Botrytis* fungus may form on the petals, eventually killing the flower.

Above: A light misting of water in the morning can help when temperatures soar.

Far left: Humidity trays are ideal to counteract a dry atmosphere.

Feeding

Most orchid mixes contain little in the way of nutrients for your plant, so you will need to feed it for best results. This is not too much of a chore if you combine it with watering. On the whole, orchids require a very weak fertilizer. Ordinary houseplant food is too potent and could cause root burn. Orchid fertilizer is available from specialist nurseries, as a powder or liquid that can be added to water. Be wary of ready-made orchid fertilizers. The amount of food required for different orchid species can vary considerably, and one dilution rate will not suit all.

Below: Feeding is best done when watering. Use orchid fertilizer and measure carefully.

There are several orchid fertilizers on the market, each with a slightly different formulation. Don't worry too much. If you find a feeding routine that works for you, stick to it. My personal preference is to use two fertilizers, one to help good plant growth, the other to aid flower production. Use the former during the spring and summer, usually coinciding with new growth, and the latter during fall and winter.

Follow the dilution instructions that come with the fertilizer and use it regularly. For most of the orchids in this book, you should feed when you water. On every fourth watering leave out the fertilizer to allow any residue to be washed from the

TIP: CHOOSING A MIX

When choosing a potting mix your best guide is to continue with the type of mix your plant has already been growing in, or ask at the orchid nursery for advice if you wish to change it. Regular houseplant soil mixes are not suitable for orchids. They may contain too much added fertilizer and do not drain quickly enough.

growing medium. Leftover solution of feed can be stored for up to two weeks in a cool, dark place or used to water other houseplants.

Repotting and growing mediums

Orchids are usually grown in well-aerated, free-draining materials. Most orchids should be repotted in the early spring, every two to three years. I wouldn't recommend repotting during the winter period, when days are short and light levels low, because most orchids are at rest and not putting out new roots. The choice of growing mediums is confusing, but can be divided into organic and non-organic. Organic mixes are made of various combinations of bark, peat, sphagnum moss, and perlite. Inorganic mixes are usually based on absorbent rockwool. Use rockwool with care—read and take heed of any guidance given on the packaging. It can be an irritant to the skin and when inhaled. Personally, I prefer not to use it, but many people grow in this medium with excellent results. Mixing organic materials with rockwool is not recommended.

Repotting with organic mixes: peat, perlite, sphagnum, bark

If your orchid is currently in a different mixture from the one you have chosen, all the old growing medium should be stripped away from the roots and any decayed or broken roots trimmed back.

If you are using the same mix, knock the plant from the pot and check to see if the mix or roots, or both, are decayed. If both are sound, continue with the potting process. If either is decayed, strip the mix away and trim any decayed or broken roots.

Choose a pot that will allow sufficient space for one year's growth. Compared with most plants, orchids usually live happily in a pot that appears to be too small. Remember that your pot should have drainage holes.

Dampen the mix (particularly sphagnum) before placing a small handful in the pot. Set your plant in position and begin filling with more mix. Tap the pot on your work surface a couple of times to ensure the mix has worked its way between the roots. When the pot has been filled to within 2 in (5 cm) of the rim, lightly firm down the compost with your fingers. Top up to about ¾ in (2 cm) from the rim.

Plants potted in sphagnum should be thoroughly watered and the mix allowed to almost dry out before watering again. It should not be necessary to water plants in peat and perlite for two to three weeks after potting, by which time the medium will have almost dried out. When

left: Once your plant is in position, fill the pot gradually with new growing medium and then gently firm it down using your fingers.

watering your orchid for the first two months, take extra care to make sure that the mix doesn't become oversaturated.

The new potting mix will contain sufficient fertilizer to encourage new growth. Once your plant has produced a significant root system, you can start using fertilizer again.

Repotting with rockwool-type growing mediums

Follow the same basic rules when preparing your orchid for repotting and for choosing a suitable pot. Wear thin gloves and a light mask when using rockwool.

Slightly dampen the rockwool (or mix) and put a small handful in the base of the pot. Position the plant so that it will be sitting on top of the mix when you have finished, about ½ in (1.5 cm) below the pot rim. With the plant in place, work the rockwool around the root system or rootball, taking care not to pot too tightly. Use just enough pressure to hold the plant in position.

Plants potted in rockwool should be watered thoroughly and never allowed to dry out completely before watering again. Because you have used an inert growing medium, it is essential to feed your orchid regularly to keep it growing healthily. If you are worried about the repotting process, many orchid nurseries will do it for a small fee.

Some orchids can be divided when they grow sufficiently large. This can rejuvenate the plant, if done correctly. Once again your nursery should be able to tell you if your orchid can be divided, what size pieces to aim for, and how and when to do it. One of the most commonly asked questions is how to divide a large *Cymbidium* and this will be dealt with in detail later (*see page 42*).

Below: Cachepots and decorative containers can be used to add style to your orchid.

Types of containers

Although many orchids grow on trees (are epiphytes), we usually grow them in a container for our convenience—it is generally far easier to manage a pot or basket than a suspended raft or tree-fern slab.

However, some orchids are sold in slatted hanging baskets, or on cork or tree-fern rafts. This method of growing has been chosen by the nursery as the easiest way to supply the orchid with its precise needs.

As a general rule, it is wise not to change the style of your orchid's growing container from a plastic pot,

To keep your moss fresh and a good color, gently mist with rainwater or filtered water.

Above: Clear pots enable you to inspect the plant's root system.

for example, to a cork raft or vice versa, without the advice of an orchid nursery. Some orchids can adapt to a change, but others most definitely cannot.

Cachepots

The majority of orchids are purchased in plastic pots, as they are very practical containers to grow them in. You may want a more stylish effect, but don't be tempted to repot into a pretty pot that doesn't allow for proper drainage.

A cachepot can be used as a decorative outer cover, but remember that most cachepots do not have drainage holes. Take care that your plant does not sit in trapped water or its roots may rot. It's best to remove your orchid when watering and then replace it when thoroughly drained.

A cachepot can be any color and material: wicker, china, clay, wood, papier-mâché, or metal. To achieve the right effect, consider both your decor and the color of the orchid flower. The top of the pot can be covered with decorative pebbles or some moss that is easily removed.

If you are going to replace the growing pot, it is best done when your orchid is out of flower as it may dislike the disturbance. Most orchids sold as houseplants come in 5 in (12 cm) pots. The moth orchid grows slowly and is likely to need repotting in a pot of the same size. A large specimen may require a 7 in (18 cm) pot. However, if the roots have been severely trimmed, a smaller pot is needed; one that fits the roots comfortably, just touching the sides, is perfect.

Other slow-growing orchids will need a container of identical size. Plants that have made obvious growth may need a larger one. It's not possible to give a precise size, as it will vary from plant to plant. The golden rule is to choose a pot to fit the roots, not the leaves, and never leave more than 1 in (3 cm) of bare growing medium around the orchid.

Ensure that your new container has adequate drainage. Unfortunately, fashion not only dictates which plant is in vogue this year, but also how to display it. Recently there has been a rise in the use of glass containers to show off orchids. These may look elegant, particularly those with moss or pretty pebbles artistically disguising the roots, but they do not make good growing containers. Unless you are very careful with watering, there's a danger of root rot. Rather than take them apart straight away, treat them with extra care. Water sparingly, but more often.

Ensure your orchid never stands in water. This may mean more frequent watering with only a small amount of water.

If your orchid is part of an arrangement in a basket, remember that baskets are inclined to leak. Water in a waterproof area—a shower stall, bath or sink is ideal.

Occasionally, you may have to remove any top dressing, such as moss or pebbles, to check that your orchid is not being overwatered.

When your orchid has finished flowering, dismantle the arrangement and grow the plants separately, repotting as needed.

Below: A variety of containers suitable for growing orchids.

If you really want to use a container with no drainage, why not use it as a cachepot? In the case of transparent materials such as glass, the outside of the growing pot can be camouflaged with decorative pebbles or moss positioned between the two containers.

Arrangements

Sometimes you will come across arrangements of several orchids that appear to be growing in a large container. In most instances, the large container is used as a cachepot to hold several smaller containers, allowing the arrangement to be taken apart quite easily. Using ferns or other small foliage plants may enhance an arrangement, but they should not be planted directly into the orchid's pot. They grow faster and more vigorously than an orchid, taking both food and water from it. Their roots may possibly become entwined, making them difficult to remove without damaging the orchid.

Above: Be careful where you position a hanging basket or raft in your home, as its surroundings will also take some of the spray.

Hanging baskets and rafts

As well as epiphytes, some terrestrial orchids (those whose home is on the ground) also look pretty displayed in a hanging basket. These varieties have naturally arching sprays of flowers. Place the plastic growing pot inside a hanging basket lined with moss or cocoa fiber. Several pots can be placed inside the same basket for effect. The orchid can be easily removed for watering and replaced when drained.

Slatted hanging baskets make suitable containers for many different orchids. Choose one made from hardwood, preferably from a sustainable source. This will last longer than softwood, which rots more quickly from watering and spraying.

Orchids growing on rafts of cork or wood can be difficult to repot and are best left alone, except for replacing the small amount of sphagnum moss that is usually tied into the roots. The moss helps to provide the plant with moisture, and renewing it each year is beneficial. Be careful where you hang your basket or raft—as both require regular spraying.

Pests and diseases

ANY BOOK THAT GIVES TIPS on looking after plants should include advice on pests and diseases. I will also look at ongoing care of your orchids in Chapter 4 (*see page 38*). Hybrid orchids on sale are usually a healthy bunch, and there are few problems with pests and diseases that you may encounter. Tough importation regulations are one reason for this. To help minimize pests and diseases of any sort, your plants need to be in a clean, airy atmosphere with suitable temperature, humidity and light levels.

If your orchid is unfortunate enough to suffer from pests or disease, the chances are you have simply been unlucky, so don't let it deter you from trying to grow another. It is worth checking what biological controls are currently available, and if you do use chemicals, take appropriate precautions. Always follow the manufacturer's instructions carefully.

Pests

Mealy bug, scale, spider mite, thrips, aphids and vine weevil have all been known to attack orchids.

Mealy bug

Mealy bugs hide in crevices of plants, often where leaves meet the stem, or at the base or on the back of petals. They can go unnoticed until they reach about ¼ in (5 mm). The flat, grayish white bugs appear slightly fluffy, like cotton wool. They can be eradicated by a suitable insecticide spray or using a biological control.

Above: Mealy bugs can occur on all parts of the plant, but are usually found where the leaves meet the stem or on the back of petals.

If you have four or more orchids, biological control could be the answer. (If you have only one or two plants, it would be quite expensive.) Biological controls can be purchased by mail order or from many garden centers and nurseries. Each sachet holds several insects that will devour your pests. In the case of mealy bug, *Cryptolaemus montrouzieri* is used. There is no need to memorize the name—just ask for mealy bug control. Follow the directions on the packet and when the *Cryptolaemus* have done their work, the predators will naturally die out through lack of food.

Although there are effective sprays, it is difficult to recommend a brand as they are constantly being tested and some previously used have have been withdrawn on health grounds. If you prefer to spray, your nursery should know what is currently recommended. Take care to follow the manufacturer's instructions closely. If you are unfortunate enough to find mealy bug on your orchid, check all your other houseplants. They love to live on tree ferns and other foliage plants.

Above: Tiny scale insects on a *Cattleya* leaf.

Scale

There are several different types of scale insects that can attack an orchid. The most common are the soft-shelled brown scale (seen on stems) and a grayish, hard-shelled scale that hides itself away like mealy bug. Scale can be picked off by hand, but this is a laborious task and the tiny, young insects are easily missed. Again, if you wish to spray, check on the current recommendations, and use with care.

Spider mite

Spider mite is less common and more difficult to spot. Red spider punctures tiny holes in both leaves and flowers. The first sign might be the hairy web that the adult makes on the underside of leaves and in which eggs are laid. On close inspection the leaves have a cloudy, silver-gray surface. The tiny false spider mite makes deep pits in the leaves that can become shriveled and distorted before dropping. Mites are far harder to eradicate than mealy bug. Nurseries use chemical sprays (acaricides), but these are not for retail sale. If you wish to spray, find out if there is anything new on the market.

Above: Red spider mite is one of the most difficult pests to spot. Look out for discoloration on the underside of leaves.

There is a biological control for red spider that you can buy, *Phytoseiulus persimilis*. Follow the directions on the packet closely. If you find this does not work, you will have to destroy the plant.

Thrips

Thrips are even smaller pests and consequently harder to spot. They chew the surfaces of flowers and sometimes leaves. Control is by chemical spray, but take advice before purchasing an insecticide.

Aphids

Aphids are attracted to some orchids, particularly to their buds. They can be washed or knocked off the plant. If you spot aphids, it is best to deal with them at once. Their tremendous rate of reproduction will lead to a serious problem if ignored.

Above: To remove aphids, swill the flowers in a bowl of water or knock the aphids off with a fine jet of water.

Vine weevil

You can detect vine weevils' presence by chunks disappearing from flowers. The adult beetle can be found on the blooms, and during repotting its larvae may be seen in the growing medium. Orchid roots do not appear to be damaged by this pest, but to protect the flowers you should purchase a systemic spray or a powder that can be dissolved and watered into your plant. If you find vine weevil, it is a good idea to treat all your houseplants to destroy the source of this pest and prevent its spread.

Others

Other pests to watch out for are slugs, snails, mice and bees (yes, bees). Although not common in the home, slugs and snails will happily munch their way through a juicy flower bud or two. Apart from the damage they cause, their presence can be detected by the slime trail they leave behind. Be careful that a slug or snail doesn't hitch a ride when bringing in an orchid from outdoors. Either pick off individual slugs and snails, or scatter suitable pellets, if appropriate.

Above: Look out for vine weevil and treat it appropriately. Protect any other houseplants, too.

Above: Although not harmful to your orchid, ants can be attracted by greenfly.

Mice are a nuisance in the fall and winter to many growers, but are less likely to be a problem inside. They are tempted by the pollen caps, which are full of protein. If you see evidence of this pest at any time, deal with it promptly.

Bees are wonderful insects, but they are not always the friend of *Cymbidium* growers. The bumble bee is attracted to *Cymbidium* flowers and is the ideal size to complete the pollination cycle. When pollination has taken place the flower collapses; its job is done.

Ants are not regular orchid pests, but they are drawn to the sticky, sweet fluid of scale insects or aphids, and the droplets of sap sometimes found on orchid stems. They should be controlled with a specific preparation, available from your garden center, to prevent them spreading pests between plants.

And finally, watch your cat! You might like orchids on the windowsill, but if your pet finds a plant in its favorite place for a snooze, it may well knock it over.

Diseases

The diseases that can affect orchids are fungal or viral.

Fungal

Fungal diseases are usually a sign of poor growing conditions, such as dank air. If your orchids are being grown in a healthy climate, you should not come across them. *Botrytis* is one of the most common fungal infections that attack orchids. This may be identified by small, black spots on the flower petals. Remove the flowers and spray with a fungicide, but the essential point is to improve the growing conditions of your plant to prevent the fungus from returning.

Other molds can attack roots and leaves. Dealing with these is the same for all fungal diseases. Remove the infected part, spray with a fungicide and, most importantly, improve your orchid's environment.

Viral

The viral infections of orchids are beyond the scope of this book and there is little that you can do. Viral disease is not simple to diagnose. If one of your plants has obvious pale (unpigmented) patches, patterning or discolorations on the flowers or leaves, this could be a viral infection. Isolate the suspect plant.

If you are within traveling distance of an orchid nursery, you could call them up and ask if they would take a look at it for you. Some of them will not want a potentially infected plant at their nursery, so do ask first. If help is not at hand, the only other check you could make is to look at the new growth. Are these leaves marked at all or is it only the old ones? If the young growth is unmarked and healthy, it is possible that your plant does not have a virus. If, on the other hand, it too is marked, the only thing to do is dispose of the plant. Throw out the pot, too, and any support or decoration that has been in contact with it. Sterilize any tools you might have used on the plant and keep a watchful eye on any orchid that has been near the diseased plant.

Chapter 3

DISPLAYING ORCHIDS IN THE HOME

Orchids will look good practically anywhere in your home, whether you choose a simple display of a single orchid or a larger arrangement containing a variety of plants. In this chapter we consider a range of tips and techniques for both the beginner and the more experienced arranger.

Planning your arrangement

A GOOD ARRANGEMENT IS LIKE A GOOD PICTURE. The container provides a frame, concentrating the eye on the important plants. It's also a decorative feature in its own right, unless completely hidden by plants, and should be considered when planning an arrangement. Check its dimensions to see how many plants it will hold comfortably and if it is deep enough to cover the growing pots. It's easy enough to raise the height of the growing pots by putting them on chunks of polystyrene, but very difficult to hide pot rims that protrude above the container.

Cachepots for arrangements have already been discussed in Chapter 2 (*see page 23*). Using your container as a cachepot means that you can easily replace a plant when it finishes flowering. Take out the pot and substitute another of similar size.

Always check the orchid profiles to make sure they are suitable for where the container will be located. If you are undecided, look through the profiles in this book for guidance (*see pages 48–140*). If your first choice is not available in flower, either due to seasonal factors or stock limitations, your nursery should be able to offer a similar alternative.

After making your purchase, check how the flower stems are supported. Moth orchids are often attached to the support cane by plastic ties or clips. These can be unobtrusive, but are sometimes crude or brightly colored and distracting. They can be replaced, for example, with raffia ties or bows. Take care not to tie too tightly or you may snap the stem.

Right: A dramatic floor standing arrangement in stoneware.

Display techniques

THE SIMPLEST DISPLAY TECHNIQUE is to place a single orchid growing in a plastic pot inside a close-fitting, decorative cachepot and top it with moss or pretty pebbles to hide the rim. Moss is readily available at nurseries and garden centers, which often have a section devoted to florist sundries. You are likely to find decorative pebbles there, too. They can be a natural color, smooth and glossy, or a brightly colored gravel, such as aquarium gravel, which can complement the orchid and your decor. From time to time, remove the decorative topping to check the dampness of the soil mix underneath. When watering, remove the topping and cachepot. After a thorough draining, reassemble your arrangement. Include decorative butterflies or colored, twisty stems to add interest if you wish.

Using foliage

Larger displays give more scope for the keen arranger. Generally, it's best to use an uneven number of plants: say, three or five orchids. They can be identical to each other, the same type, or all different—but choose plants that have the same growing needs. The selection of foliage plants is wide, but they should be in proportion with the display. Two or three small pots of the same fern, rather than one large one, will be easier to handle and position. Regular trimming prevents ivies from outgrowing their allotted space. Positioning each plant pot to your satisfaction may take a little time.

Try to hide the pot rims, perhaps with ferns whose natural shape and growth habit make them ideal for this job. Ferns need regular misting to keep them looking good, so take care not to spray surrounding furnishings at the same time. Another way to disguise pot rims is to use cocoa fiber, which looks good with larger plants, such as *Cymbidium*. It does not rot, is easily removed for maintenance and can be reused.

Above: A moth orchid displayed in a glass cube.

Hanging baskets

Orchids that look good displayed in hanging baskets have naturally arching flower stems, for example, *Cymbidium* Sarah Jean, or a growth habit that is not suited to a regular pot. Here's a way to put your creative

abilities to good use. Line a plastic-coated wire or metal hanging basket with a thick layer of moss. This is purely for decorative effect. Use one large plant with several spikes in the center and gently arrange the flower stems so they fall naturally all around the basket. If you are using several smaller plants, space them evenly around the basket and angled slightly toward the rim. This can be achieved by propping up the pots with small chunks of polystyrene or oasis. Finally, fill in any space with expanded clay pebbles and top off with more moss.

Ready-made displays

Your orchid may already be displayed in a container and all you will need to do is select the position where it will be most happy. Refer to the plant profiles and consider its temperature, light and humidity requirements. If you choose an arrangement for a particular spot and find that it isn't the best place for the orchid, either site it somewhere else—where it may not look as good, but will thrive—or place it exactly where you intended and be prepared for the plant to have a shorter life span.

Trays

In a dry atmosphere, place a plant on a moist gravel tray to help increase humidity. A gravel tray also provides room for several orchids and other decorative houseplants, such as ferns and ivies, to be displayed.

First, choose your tray. It doesn't have to be one of those drab horticultural plastic affairs; it can be quite dramatic. I have used glass, china, plastic and metal (not iron, though) successfully. The tray should be at least 3 in (8 cm) deep and tall enough to hide the whole pot if you wish. It may be wise to check the effect that water has on the tray in the long term. Some metals react with water and change color, not always attractively.

Fill the bottom of the tray with a 2 in (5 cm) layer of pebbles, colored gravel or hydroleca. Place your orchid pots on top of this. To keep the bottom of an orchid pot from touching the water, position upturned saucers, or something similar, among the pebbles, to keep the pot bottoms above the water level.

If you are using several orchids and foliage plants, take the time to position each plant pot to your satisfaction. First, put in the orchids on their bases, if necessary. Stagger them slightly—nature rarely uses straight lines.

Next, position your foliage plants. Ivy will look good trailing over the edge of the tray, and small ferns can be clustered around the orchid pots. This not only provides a suitable microclimate for your orchids, but also hides the plant pots. When you are satisfied, fill with 1½ in (4 cm) of water and remember to top this up regularly. Remove the plant pots when you need to water and feed your orchids. They can easily be slotted back into the display after draining. Occasionally, take apart the whole display and thoroughly clean the tray to avoid any "tide marks" or algae buildup.

Right: This tray has first been lined with a thick layer of plastic sheeting to waterproof it. Cover the base with pebbles or gravel.

Left: Take care positioning each plant until you are satisfied with the final result.

Where to display your orchid

T HERE ARE AS MANY PLACES TO DISPLAY orchids as there are possibilities for using them on special occasions—weddings, holidays and dinner parties, to name but a few. A display or arrangement will look attractive practically anywhere in your home. Displays will be governed by the space available and your own lifestyle. However, you should be wary of keeping orchids in rooms that are drafty or have low levels of light.

Kitchens and bathrooms

Initially, kitchens and bathrooms spring to mind as good places to display orchids because they are usually warm and humid. However, bathrooms are probably the least favorable place—they often have small windows, with frosted glass, and light levels are very low. Some heating systems are timed to go off, or at least operate at a low level, when the room is not in use. The cool building materials used in modern bathrooms quickly lose heat, which could leave your orchid decidedly chilly. I have successfully kept an arrangement of *Zygopetalum* in my own bathroom, but it has very large sash windows that provide ample light and a permanently heated towel rail.

Kitchens are generally a better prospect. They are often the warmest room in the house and may have deep windowsills. Many orchids can thrive here, given the right aspect. Just make sure it has enough room among the clutter that usually graces so many kitchen windowsills. Single plants of moth orchids or *Dendrobium* could be grown here successfully. If you have a large kitchen with a dining table or breakfast bar, you may have room for an arrangement. A single moth orchid, tied with raffia and displayed in a wicker basket or plain wooden cachepot, could look great.

Below: A windowsill can provide an ideal spot for your orchids, as long as they are out of direct sunlight.

Right: In a warm room with limited shelf space, a mini *Cattleya* could be an ideal choice.

Bedrooms

Bedrooms provide ample opportunities for displaying orchids. Soft furnishings retain heat for some time after it is switched off. A cool, tailored room might provide the ideal setting for a *Paphiopedilum*, such as Hellas, and a simple maidenhair fern, arranged in a polished wood container.

A modern bedroom with clean lines and pure colors could sport a long, low, rectangular black or solid-colored container filled with a row of white moth orchids. Top it off with colored gravel that complements the room's color scheme. An arrangement of several identical *Cymbidium* in a wicker basket would add a touch of luxury to any bedroom. If the furnishings are traditional, then some draping around the basket might be a perfect finishing touch.

As spare bedrooms are not in constant use, I feel arrangements are wasted there. However, I always have a couple of simple moth orchid arrangements around the house ready to move into spare bedrooms when visitors arrive. One is usually in glass (used as a cachepot) with irregular layers of moss and colored gravel. The other is in a zinc container, topped with moss and pebbles. They are easily adapted for special occasions, such as Christmas, by adding a bow or a white, sparkly butterfly. Spare bedrooms also make perfect homes for cool-growing orchids when they are out of flower.

Hallways and landings
Hallways and landings vary greatly in shape, size and temperature. For those lucky enough to have room for a side table, a basket of several *Oncidium* Sweet Sugar would make a cheerful, welcoming display. If you have room for a pedestal, then an arrangement of miniature *Cymbidium* in a simple, classic container with trailing *tradescantia*, would look stunning. Setting it in front of a hall mirror creates the effect of doubling the amount of orchids in your display.

Living and dining rooms
Living rooms usually have a coffee table or a side table. Any of the warmer-growing orchids would be happy here. The favorite house orchid, the moth orchid, is an obvious choice. Search out colors that suit your decor, rather than the usual white or bright pink. For a taller arrangement, consider using *Vuylstekeara* or *Beallara*, both long-

Left: *Dendrobium* Stardust graces a hall table.

lasting. An open fireplace that you don't use during the summer is an ideal position for a *Miltassia*. The large fireplace in my living room is no longer used for heating, but it makes the perfect frame for a large standard *Cymbidium*. This is now a regular part of my traditional Christmas decorations, and although the high heat levels mean it does not flower as long as it might, its magnificent appearance is always remarked upon.

Dining rooms have the advantage of a table to position a display. Often kept cooler than the living room, a dining room may be ideal for the pansy orchid, *Miltoniopsis*, for example. It takes up little space and gives the added bonus of fragrance in the morning. You could display the floating flowers of *Cymbidium* in a round dish at the center of your dining-room table, or create a tall centerpiece for a special dinner party using a medium-tall metal pedestal topped with *Cymbidium* Sarah Jean. Let it trail down with *Tradescantia* and creeping fig.

Right: A simple ceramic cube provides a perfect foil for this mantel.

Chapter 4

COMMON CONCERNS AND SIMPLE SOLUTIONS

There are some minor worries that often occur when growing orchids in the home. Most of these can be effectively dealt with by using one of the simple solutions or procedures described here.

A moth orchid stops flowering

As soon as the flowers die, cut the stem back just above a node (*see diagram*), leaving about 10–12 in (25–30 cm) of stem. Often, a secondary spike, or flower stem, is produced from this node, and new flowers will appear after two to three months. Do not "rest" your moth orchid or change its routine.

Unlike other orchids, the moth orchid does not have an annual rhythm; it may produce flower spikes at any time of the year. Should a large, healthy plant fail to produce a flower spike in a reasonable amount of time (eight to ten months), reduce the temperature by 10°F (5°C) for four weeks to encourage flowering.

This procedure does not apply to other types of orchids whose stems are usually cut down near to the base.

Above: Cut just above the node on a moth orchid stem to encourage quick reflowering.

A moth orchid has untidy roots spilling out of its pot

These are called aerial roots, which the orchid grows to absorb moisture from the atmosphere. In the case of the moth orchid, they should be gray and worm-like. If the roots are withered, brown or flat (or all three), they are useless to the plant. Neatly removing them is recommended. If the roots are healthy, but unattractive, check that the plant has a good root system inside its pot before you do any tidying. You must leave enough roots to take up water and ensure healthy growth. Other orchids that have aerial roots would not be able to cope with trimming like this.

If the moth orchid's aerial roots are dried out and dead, an increase in humidity is required. First, check that it is not positioned too close to a radiator or other heat source, then consider putting it on a moist gravel tray or grouping several plants together to form a more humid microclimate.

Above: Aerial roots on an *Oncidium* can look unsightly when they spill out over the top of the pot.

The orchid grows a "baby" plant on one of its branches

This is a young orchid plantlet, known as a keiki. If you wish to try to cultivate it, be patient; it takes several years for the young plant to grow large enough to flower.

Wait until the keiki has produced a small root system, and then carefully cut through the supporting stem about 2 mm either side of the plantlet. Take a tiny pot, about 2 in (5 cm) wide, and put a little damp growing medium, preferably sphagnum moss, in the bottom. Hold the plantlet gently in place and fill with growing medium. Ensure it has worked its way between the roots. Water thoroughly, drain and place in a small heated propagator or frame. The propagator should be in a shady spot and be well ventilated. Plant propagators can be purchased at nursery centers; they are commonly used to propagate seeds or cuttings that need a little extra heat and humidity to encourage growth. Although they're a relatively inexpensive tool for the gardener, you may not want to buy one for a single keiki.

Below: A *Dendrobium nobile* with keikis growing at the end of one of its branches. Remove the keiki once it has developed its own root system.

Keep the plantlet in a daytime temperature of 68°–75°F (20°–24°C) and around 64°F (18°C) at night, comfortably warm. The most important thing to remember is not to allow it to dry out completely. For the first couple of weeks, water without feeding every four to seven days.

By the third week, the plantlet will require feeding, as it should have produced a new root system. Begin using a very diluted orchid food. When the plant has established a strong root system, probably after three to four months, begin feeding at the recommended strength.

For the first couple of weeks, no ventilation should be needed. After that, it will be necessary to ventilate a little during the day. Raise the lid of your propagator about ½ in (1.5 cm) in the morning to stop extensive buildup of moisture. Increase the ventilation after about six weeks.

After six months your keiki should have become large enough to be potted into fresh growing medium. A moth orchid keiki would benefit from being left in the propagator for as long as 18 months, if possible.

A moth orchid doesn't stop flowering

If you have one like this, you are fortunate. Some varieties of *Phalaenopsis* seem to flower constantly. Make sure that you feed your plant regularly, as it will need some extra help. If the leaves are beginning to look stressed, but the plant has a good root system, you might consider sacrificing the flowers. Cut the stem(s) to ½ in (1.5 cm) above the base to let it recover its vigor. If you can't bring yourself to do this, just enjoy your orchid. It might die of exhaustion, but it will give you a great deal of pleasure.

Above: *Phalaenopsis* Brother Sara Gold has long-lasting flowers.

The orchid has a wonderful flower spike but has lost all of its leaves

There are some varieties of orchid that do lose their leaves each year—but not the *Phalaenopsis*, or moth orchid. Its leaves will not regrow. The plant is making a last desperate effort to reproduce itself by putting all its energy into flowering to attract a pollinator. Your plant will not look particularly attractive without leaves. You could cut the flower stem off, put it in a vase of water to enjoy, and throw away the old root system.

Getting a **Cymbidium** *to reflower*

The most common mistake is to keep a *Cymbidium* indoors all year round. A *Cymbidium* must have good light and a noticeable dip in nighttime temperatures during the summer. A drop of about 15°F (8°C) every night for a couple of weeks is required. Usually, it is not possible to get that sort of fluctuation inside our homes. If possible, put the plant outside or in an unheated greenhouse after any danger of frost has passed. Raise the pot off the ground by placing a brick underneath to help any excess water drain away, and to deter slugs or snails. Watering outside will depend on the weather. During a rainy spell, little if any is needed. If the sun shines, then your orchid will require regular watering. Take care to acclimatize your plant to outside conditions, particularly strong light. Put it in a semi-shaded position and gradually increase light levels by a few hours per day. Bring the plant back indoors in the fall, before the first frosts arrive. Acclimatize it gradually at this time, too—a sudden burst of heat could result in bud drop.

If you have done this and there is still no sign of a flower stem, take a good look at the leaves. If they look healthy, lush and green, the orchid is putting all its efforts into producing leaves instead of flowers. Stop fertilizing it for six months—your orchid is probably receiving too much nitrogen.

If the leaves are sickly green and your orchid looks poorly, check the roots for signs of overwatering or underwatering, and the leaves for pests. If these look fine, perhaps your orchid needs feeding. Although *Cymbidium* can tolerate some neglect, they need a certain amount of attention to keep them happy.

Finally, consider when your plant was last repotted. Some *Cymbidium* miss a year if repotting is carried out late in the season, and if divided, it will almost certainly skip a flowering season. If the new divisions were too small, it could take several years to recover.

Above: Miniature *Cymbidium* King's Loch 'Cooksbridge' flowers during the winter.

After flowering, the large, floppy leaves of a **Cymbidium** *look untidy*
These leaves might not look very elegant, but they are needed to make food for the plant. They will not regrow, so they should not be cut back. As this is the time when the plant can be put outside, at least you won't have to look at a pot full of unattractive leaves in the house.

Dividing a large **Cymbidium**
Examine your plant and you will see a group of green, thickened, "bulb-like" stems (pseudobulbs) and probably some older brown ones. Don't be tempted to split the plant into single pseudobulbs. Although it is possible to grow on each one and produce flowering plants, this would take about seven years! What you should aim for is at least three green pseudobulbs and an old brown one to each division.

Equip yourself with some growing medium, the correct number of pots (which will be a lot smaller in size) and a sturdy knife. Remove the plant from its pot. You will be confronted with a mass of roots. Carefully slice

through the plant to divide it, trying not to cut through the pseudobulbs, but between them. If you damage a pseudobulb, either remove it or dust it with an approved fungicidal powder. Leave only one brown pseudobulb attached to each piece to act as a food reserve, and throw away the rest.

Next, examine the roots of each piece; they should be plump and wormlike. If they are at all damaged, soft and brown, or flat and shriveled, you should adjust your watering regime in the future. Strip off all of the old growing medium, any damaged roots and cut pieces. Trim back the remaining roots to about 5 in (12 cm).

The new pots should be just big enough for two years' growth—the width of each piece plus an extra 1 in (3 cm). Put a handful of dampened growing medium in the bottom of the pot and then hold the plant in place, positioning it to leave room for new growth. This will come from the green parts of the plant, not the brown. Fill around the plant, tapping gently on your work surface to settle the growing medium around the roots. The pseudobulbs should be sitting on the surface of the growing medium, which should reach nearly to the rim of the pot. Water thoroughly from the top.

It is usual for divided plants to miss the next couple of flowering seasons. If you use large pots or divide into small pieces, the wait could be even longer.

Sticky droplets appear on the stem of an orchid
These are beads of sap that are sometimes produced if a plant is under stress; often there is nothing you can do. Just watch out for ants that might be attracted by the sap. Ants do not harm orchids, but they can spread disease from one plant to another.

Bud drop
Bud drop has several causes, the most common of which is shock. This could have been caused by poor wrapping when purchased or by moving your plant abruptly from a cool spot to a much warmer one (or vice versa). A dry atmosphere or a draft can also induce stress in plants. In most cases, your plant is likely to recover, but you will have to wait for a new flower spike. Check the orchid's position for drafts and, if a dry atmosphere was the cause, increase the humidity by placing the plant pot on a damp gravel tray.

Folded leaves on a pansy orchid or Odontoglossum
The plant has had a period of "stop–start" growing, which has resulted in this folded or "concertinaed" look. One possible cause is fluctuating humidity. Try placing the plant pot on a damp gravel tray to increase humidity levels.

Another possible cause could be root problems. Turn the plant upside down and remove its pot. Check for pests or root damage. The roots should be solid and look like thin worms. If they are brown or black and squishy, or flat and dried up, then you have been overwatering or underwatering. To save the plant, remove the damaged roots and repot into a much smaller pot. Choose a pot to fit the roots, not the plant, snugly, and adjust your watering accordingly.

An orchid looks top-heavy in its pot

Many orchids look as if they are tight in their pot. They prefer it this way, and it is much easier to regulate watering. Check the growing guide to see how often your orchid needs to be repotted.

Another reason to have a small pot might be because your plant has a small root system. When repotting an orchid, old damaged roots are stripped away, leaving the plant with fewer roots. Pot size is guided by the size of the roots, not the size of the plant. Roots have a better chance of recovery in a small pot. If the plant is in danger of toppling over, place it inside a cachepot for stability.

Browning and loss of leaves

Like most plants, your orchid will lose a leaf from time to time, and this is quite natural. However, if an orchid loses many leaves, it probably has a root problem (see page 41). This is not the case with deciduous orchids that shed their leaves naturally as part of their growing cycle.

Growing from a seedpod

It's not unusual for an orchid to produce a seedpod—probably the result of being visited by insects that carried out the pollination. Each pod produces thousands, if not millions, of seeds. This is nature's way of assuring reproduction, as only one or two will find suitable conditions to germinate. Orchid seed can only germinate in the presence of a particular fungus, reproduced commercially in the laboratory. The fungus is found in the growing mix around the mother plant, and nurseries used to sow seed in the same pot as the mother plant. With luck, one or two seeds germinated.

However, growing from a seedpod is a tricky business and even if a seed did germinate, it would be many years before it would be a flowering- sized plant. My advice is to throw the pod away.

Taking cuttings from an orchid

Most orchids cannot be propagated by cuttings. Stem cuttings from a *Phalaenopsis* will not work outside laboratory conditions. However, if you have a Jewel orchid, *Ludisia*, sections can be cut from its stems and potted up. When plants are large enough, some orchids like the Slipper orchid, *Paphiopedilum*, or the *Cymbidium* can be divided.

Placing your orchid outside during fine weather

This depends on the type of orchid you have and where you live. In warm climates, *Cymbidium* can be grown outside all year round, while in others it would go out only over the summer to help the production of flower stems.

In the warmer regions of the U.S. and Australia, the occasional shower of warm rain can be beneficial to the moth orchid. However, in the U.K. it should not be put outside at all. The same applies to *Cattleya*. In general, if an orchid was sold to you as a houseplant, keep it indoors unless the instructions say otherwise.

Planting orchids and ferns together

It is better not to plant orchids and ferns together in one pot. Orchids need a more free-draining growing medium than most other houseplants and, on the whole, they do not need to be watered as frequently. Most ferns enjoy a damp soil all the time. Most orchid roots need to dry out between waterings. Also, orchids like their roots to be quite constricted, and a large root run would not be ideal. The ferns would compete for space, water and food—and would win.

The solution is to place the plants in individual pots inside one large one and cover the surface with moss, pebbles or cocoa fiber to hide the pot rims. This gives the same effect as a mixed planting, and the surface covering can be easily removed to water individual plants.

Leaving your orchid when you're away

Two weeks should be no problem; a month would require help from a neighbor or friend. Any longer than this and it might be wise to board your plants with someone who knows how to care for them properly.

If you are away for two weeks or less, thoroughly water your orchids, drain and leave them together in a shady spot. If anyone is going to be visiting your home when you're away, warn them not to water the orchids.

If you are going away for a month, ask a friend or neighbor to come in after two weeks and check if your orchids need watering. Remember to tell them the old maxim for orchid watering: if in doubt—DON'T!

If your vacation is for longer than a month, try to enlist the help of a fellow grower, who should appreciate their needs. Alternatively, look for an orchid-boarding service. Many nurseries provide this, but remember to check the fees, as it can be expensive.

Right: Miniature *Cymbidium* Samares will be happy for a couple of weeks while you are away on vacation.

Chapter 5

DIRECTORY

The range of orchids available today is enormous. As well as countless species, there are thousands of registered hybrids to choose from. This selection has been made to include plants, both common and more unusual, that are widely available at orchid nurseries and will happily grow in most homes.

Angraecum sesquipedale

This is an orchid of historical significance and is also easy to grow. Its common name is the Comet orchid. Although smaller plants may flower readily and grow on a windowsill, mature specimens can reach up to 3 ft (1 m). Plants have leathery leaves and stiff aerial roots growing from the stem. In late winter or spring, the flower spikes appear, each with five or six large blooms. The extraordinary, star-shaped flowers of creamy white are waxy in texture and have a long spur more than 12 in (30 cm) long, designed by nature to attract a single pollinator, a hawkmoth. Consequently, the spicy perfume is stronger at night to entice the moth.

INDOOR CARE

Temperature: It grows best in daytime temperatures above 68°F (20°C), with nights not below 60°F (16°C). It loves an airy position. Avoid placing too close to a radiator or in a draft.

Light: A light spot is best, but not in full, noonday sun. Afternoon sun is ideal. Small plants enjoy a west-facing window.

Watering: Water freely from the top when the growing medium is almost dry, but never let it dry out completely. Always allow the plant to drain thoroughly. Water is also absorbed from the atmosphere by the aerial roots outside the pot.

Humidity: Comet orchids enjoy an airy position, but the higher the temperature, the more humidity is needed. In a dry atmosphere, place the pot on a moist gravel tray to help prevent leaf tips from browning. Gently mist the leaves early in the morning if temperatures are above 68°F (20°C).

Feeding: Include orchid fertilizer in three out of four waterings.

Potting: It resents being disturbed; repotting should usually be carried out directly after flowering and only when the pot is completely full of roots. Take care not to snap off the aerial roots.

After flowering: When the flowers die, cut the stem back, leaving about 1 in (3 cm). Continue the watering and feeding regime all year, but reduce the frequency as temperatures fall.

> **TIP** Before repotting the plant, soak the roots in warm water for up to 10 minutes to make them less brittle.

Historical note: When Charles Darwin saw the Comet orchid he predicted from its unusually long spur and nocturnal scent that a very long-tongued moth or similar night-flying insect must be its natural pollinator. Many years later, Darwin was proved entirely correct, by the discovery of the hawkmoth, *Xanthopan morganii praedicta*, which pollinates this orchid.

Beallara Peggy Ruth Carpenter

This orchid belongs to the *Odontoglossum* family. Each flower spike carries four or more blooms that last between four and six weeks. It flowers about every 10 months, usually in the spring or summer. Some aerial roots can be seen above the growing medium. It is an established favorite and reliable pot plant.

INDOOR CARE

Temperature: This tolerant plant prefers daytime temperatures of 68°F (20°C), but it can survive in temperatures up to 84°F (29°C), with nights not below 55°F (13°C). Avoid placing too close to a radiator or in a draft.

Light: A north- or west-facing window is ideal. It does not like direct sunlight.

Watering: Never allow the plant to dry out completely. Water thoroughly from the top when the growing medium is almost dry and allow to drain. Do not let the plant sit in water.

Humidity: If you live in a dry atmosphere, stand the plant on a moist gravel tray to create a humid microclimate and assist growth. Gently misting the leaves early in the morning if the air is dry also helps.

Feeding: Include orchid fertilizer in three out of four waterings.

Potting: This should usually be carried out every other year. Repot when you can see 2–3 in (5–8 cm) of new growth.

After flowering: When the flowers die, cut the stem back to about 1 in (3 cm). Continue the watering and feeding regime all year.

> **TIP** If a large, healthy plant fails to produce a flower spike within a reasonable time (about 10 months), reduce the temperature by 10°F (5°C) for four weeks to encourage flowering.

Beallara Tahoma Glacier

Another member of the *Odontoglossum* family, this is a modern hybrid and reliable pot plant. Its flower spike carries nine or more translucent, off-white and red patterned flowers, which can last a month or more. Flowering takes place about every 10 months, usually during the spring and summer. Some aerial roots can be seen above the growing medium.

An enthusiastic grower, it will develop into a large multi-spiked plant given the correct care.

Other *Beallara* to consider: Tropic Splendor, Marfitch, and many more.

INDOOR CARE

Temperature: *Beallara* is quite tolerant and can be grown in daytime temperatures up to 84°F (29°C), with nights not below 55°F (13°C). Avoid placing too close to a radiator or in a draft.

Light: A north- or west-facing window is ideal. It does not like direct sunlight.

Watering: Never allow the plant to dry out completely. Water thoroughly from the top when the growing medium is almost dry and allow to drain. Never let your plant sit in water.

Humidity: If you live in a dry atmosphere, stand the plant on a moist gravel tray to create a humid microclimate and assist growth. Gently misting the leaves early in the morning if the air is dry also helps.

Feeding: Include orchid fertilizer in three out of four waterings.

Potting: This is usually done every other year. Repot when you can see 2–3 in (5–8 cm) of new growth.

After flowering: When the flowers die, cut the stem back to about 1 in (3 cm). Continue the watering and feeding regime all year.

> **TIP** If a large, healthy plant fails to produce a flower spike within a reasonable time (about 10 months), reduce the temperature by 10°F (5°C) for four weeks to encourage flowering.

Bletilla formosana

This orchid can be grown outdoors in a sheltered spot, away from midday sun. In the fall, plant the corm-like pseudobulbs 2 in (5 cm) deep. In colder areas (where temperatures can fall to 14°F (–8°C)), plant more deeply: about 4–6 in (10–15 cm) deep. In spring, the flower stems appear from inside the young shoots, and at this time water freely. Produces up to 10 rose-pink/magenta flowers on a spike. After flowering, the leaves of *Bletilla* die down for winter. If it is protected from severe frosts, it can be left in the ground all year.

Other *Bletilla* to consider: Yokohama and the Penrose series.

INDOOR CARE

Temperature: They grow best in daytime temperatures below 64°F (18°C), with cool nights below 55°F (13°C). Avoid placing the plant close to a heat source. It can also be grown in an alpine house.

Light: An east-facing window is ideal.

Watering: Water the growing medium from the top when it is almost dry and allow the plant to drain. Water freely when the flower spikes appear, but don't let the pot stand in water for more than 10 minutes at a time.

Feeding: Feed after flowering until the leaves begin to die down. Use a quarter-strength, water-soluble garden fertilizer.

Potting: This should usually be done every year to freshen the growing medium. Plant pseudobulbs in the fall, after the leaves have died down and before new growth emerges.

After flowering: Allow a cool rest period during the winter, but continue to water about every four weeks to prevent the bulb from shriveling.

Brassada Orange Delight

This compact hybrid produces spikes of 10 or more brilliantly colored, spidery flowers. Their base color is usually a stunning orange or orangey-yellow, accentuated by occasional dark patterning. Summer flowering, it holds its blooms in good condition for over a month. You might like to stake the lower half of the spike, or leave it free-growing to show off its arching habit. This orchid is a good alternative when a *Brassia* would be too large.

Other *Brassada* to consider: Mem. Bert Field, Mivada.

INDOOR CARE

Temperature: *Brassada* grow in daytime temperatures of up to 84°F (29°C), with nights not below 54°F (12°C). Avoid placing it close to a radiator or in a draft.

Light: A west-facing window is ideal. Likes good light, but not direct sunlight.

Watering: Never allow the mix to dry out completely. Water thoroughly from the top when it is almost dry and allow to drain.

Humidity: If you live in a dry atmosphere, stand the plant on a moist gravel tray to create a microclimate and assist growth. Gently misting the leaves early in the morning if the air is really dry also helps.

Feeding: Include orchid fertilizer in three out of four waterings.

Potting: This should usually be done every other year in the spring. Repot when you can see 2–3 in (5–8 cm) of new growth emerging from the base of the plant. Choose an orchid growing mix that includes medium-grade bark.

After flowering: When the flowers die, cut the stem back to about ½ in (1.5 cm). Continue the watering and feeding regime all year.

Brassia verrucosa

Brassia verrucosa is commonly known as the Spider orchid, as each spike carries up to nine cream or pale green, spidery flowers, which can last for over a month on the plant during the spring and summer. Some aerial roots can be seen above the growing medium. Take care to position your plant so that it has enough room for its spike to develop naturally. Stake only the lower half of the flower spike to allow it to arch gracefully.

INDOOR CARE

Temperature: The plant grows best in daytime temperatures up to 84°F (29°C), with nights not below 55°F (13°C). Although it is fairly tolerant, avoid placing it too close to a radiator or in a draft.

Light: A west-facing window is ideal. It does not like direct sunlight.

Watering: Water regularly and never let the plant dry out completely. Water thoroughly from the top when the growing medium is almost dry and allow to drain.

Humidity: If you live in a dry atmosphere, stand the plant on a moist gravel tray to create a microclimate and assist growth. Gently misting the leaves early in the morning if the air is dry also helps.

Feeding: Include orchid fertilizer in three out of four waterings.

Potting: The plant does not like to be disturbed. Repot every two to three years when the growing medium needs renewing. Choose a growing medium that includes some bark in the mix. This is best carried out in the spring when you can see 2–3 in (5–8 cm) of new growth from the base of the plant.

After flowering: When the flowers die, cut the stem back to about 1 in (3 cm). Continue the watering and feeding regime all year.

Brassolaeliocattleya Abbeville

This member of the *Cattleya* family usually flowers in the late winter or early spring, with blooms that last for up to four weeks. Aerial roots can be seen developing above the growing medium.

INDOOR CARE

Temperature: These plants grow best in daytime temperatures of 68°–84°F (20°–29°C), with nights not below 57°F (14°C). Avoid placing too close to a radiator or in a draft.

Light: They thrive in good light, but need protection from full, midday sun. An east- or west-facing window works well.

Watering: Water the plant frequently when growing, but allow it to dry out a little between waterings. Water thoroughly from the top and allow to drain. Reduce the frequency of watering as the temperature drops and light levels decrease. A drying-out period of about three months over the winter is beneficial. During this time, water about every six weeks. Even if your plant is in flower, it does not need more water. Gradually increase watering in the spring to encourage new growth.

Humidity: Good humidity is the key to success. The higher the temperature, the higher the humidity required. In a dry atmosphere, stand the plant on a moist gravel tray to create a microclimate and assist growth.

 TIP This plant loves an airy atmosphere.

Feeding: Include orchid fertilizer in three out of four waterings.

Potting: Repot using a medium-coarse bark every two to three years during the spring when new growth is beginning. When the plant is large enough, it can be divided into pieces with a minimum of three bulbs to each division.

After flowering: Remove dead flowers and sheaths.

Brassolaeliocattleya Sweet Honey

Cattleya and their relations usually bloom in the spring or fall, depending on the variety. Their wonderfully fragrant flowers can last for up to four weeks. Aerial roots can be seen developing above the growing medium.

Other *Brassolaeliocattleya* to consider: Alma Kee, Greenwich, Magnificent Obsession, Waikiki Sunset, and many more.

INDOOR CARE

Temperature: The plant grows best in daytime temperatures of 68°–84°F (20°–29°C), with nights not below 57°F (14°C). Avoid placing too close to a radiator or in a draft.

Light: It thrives in good light, but needs protection from full, midday sun. It can be grown near an east- or west-facing window.

Watering: Water frequently when the plant is growing, but allow it to dry out a little between waterings. Water thoroughly from the top and allow to drain. Reduce frequency of watering as the temperature drops and light levels decrease. During the winter when a drying-out period of two to three months is beneficial, the plant should be watered about every six weeks, even if it is in flower. Gradually increase watering in the spring to encourage new growth.

Humidity: Good humidity is the key to success. The higher the temperature, the higher the humidity required. In a dry atmosphere, stand the plant on a moist gravel tray to create a microclimate and assist growth.

> **TIP** This plant loves an airy atmosphere.

Feeding: Include orchid fertilizer in three out of four waterings.

Potting: This should generally be carried out every two to three years in spring when new growth is beginning to appear. Use a medium-coarse bark. When the plant is large enough, it can be divided into pieces with a minimum of three bulbs to each division.

After flowering: Remove dead flowers and sheaths.

Burrageara Nelly Isler

This member of the *Odontoglossum* family produces spikes of attractive and long-lasting red flowers, often remaining in good condition for more than two months. It is an ideal pot plant for a centrally heated home. Sometimes aerial roots can be seen outside the pot. A plant may have two or more stems, depending on age.

Other *Burrageara* to consider: Stefan Isler, Dee Luce, Durham Wild.

INDOOR CARE

Temperature: It prefers daytime temperatures of 68°F (20°F), with nights not below 55°F (13°C). Although fairly tolerant, it will struggle in temperatures above 77°F (25°C). Avoid placing it too close to a radiator or in a draft.

Light: An east- or west-facing window is ideal.

Watering: Water the growing medium thoroughly from the top when it is almost dry and allow it to drain. Do not let it dry out completely. Take care that water does not lodge between the leaves and the pseudobulbs.

> **TIP** If water does lodge between the leaves and pseudobulbs, dab lightly with some twisted tissue to soak up the excess.

Humidity: The higher the temperature, the higher the humidity required. If you live in a dry atmosphere, stand the plant on a moist gravel tray to create a microclimate and assist growth.

Feeding: Include orchid fertilizer in three out of four waterings.

Potting: Ideally, this should be carried out every other year in the spring or early fall, but not when it is in flower.

After flowering: When the flowers die, cut back the stems to about 1 in (3 cm). Continue the watering and feeding regime until winter approaches. When the temperatures start to drop, reduce the frequency of watering.

Calanthe discolor

This semi-evergreen orchid can be grown outdoors in a sheltered spot. It usually blooms in spring or early summer. The sweetly scented flowers have white lower lips with pale to chocolate-brown petals and sepals. Some blooms may also have a hint of pink.

INDOOR CARE

Temperature: The plant grows best in daytime temperatures below 64°F (18°C), with cool nights below 50°F (10°C). Avoid placing it too close to a heat source. The plant can also be grown in an alpine house.

Light: An east-facing window is ideal, but keep away from full sunlight.

Watering: Water the plant thoroughly from the top when almost dry and allow it to drain. Never let the growing medium dry out completely; keep it damp, but not waterlogged.

Humidity: The higher the temperature, the higher the humidity required. If you live in a dry atmosphere, stand the plant on a moist gravel tray to create a microclimate and assist growth.

Feeding: Include orchid fertilizer in three out of four waterings when in active growth.

Potting: Repot every year at the first sign of new growth.

After flowering: When the flowers die, cut back the stems to about 1 in (3 cm). Reduce the frequency of watering as temperatures start to drop.

Cattleya Valentine

Cattleya are among the most flamboyant of orchids and are often used as corsages. Their flowers can last for up to four weeks on the plant. Epiphytic roots can be seen developing above the growing medium. Other *Cattleya* to consider: Hawaiian Wedding Song, Ruth Gee, Angel Walker.

INDOOR CARE

Temperature: *Cattleya* prefers daytime temperatures above 68°F (20°C), with nights not below 57°F (14°C). Avoid placing too close to a radiator or in a draft.

Light: It thrives in good light, but needs protection from full, midday sun. An east- or west-facing window is ideal.

Watering: Water the plant frequently when growing, but allow it to dry out a little between waterings. Water thoroughly from the top and allow it to drain. Reduce the frequency of watering as the temperature drops and light levels decrease. During the winter a drying-out period of two to three months is beneficial. During this time, only water the plant about every six weeks, even if it is in flower. Gradually increase watering in the spring to encourage new growth.

Humidity: Good humidity is the key to success. The higher the temperature, the higher the humidity required. In a dry atmosphere, stand the plant on a moist gravel tray to create a microclimate and assist growth.

 TIP This plant loves an airy atmosphere.

Feeding: Include orchid fertilizer in three out of four waterings.

Potting: This should generally be carried out every two to three years in the spring when new growth is beginning. Use a medium-coarse bark. When the plant is large enough, divide it into pieces with a minimum of three bulbs in each division.

After flowering: Remove dead flowers and sheaths.

Coelogyne cristata

This delightful plant (commonly known as String of Pearls) can be grown in either a pot or slatted wooden basket. Flowering may occur when the plant is small; each stem produces a drooping spray of four or five fragrant flowers, but it might require some encouragement to get into a flowering rhythm. At maturity, the plant can reach up to 30 in (75 cm) in diameter, bearing masses of flowers in late winter and early spring. At this size, it will look its best when displayed in a large wooden hanging basket.

INDOOR CARE

Temperature: The plant grows best in temperatures up to 64°F (18°C), with nights not below 50°F (10°C). Avoid placing too close to a radiator or in a draft.

Light: An east-facing window is ideal. Keep the plant away from full sunlight.

Watering: Water liberally when the first shoots appear from the base of the plant and drain thoroughly. Never allow the plant to sit in water, as this could rot the tender shoots.

Humidity: The higher the temperature, the higher the humidity required. If you live in a dry atmosphere, stand the pot on a moist gravel tray to create a microclimate and assist growth. If the plant is large enough for a hanging basket, regular misting during the morning will help prevent the leaf tips from browning.

Feeding: Include orchid fertilizer in three out of four waterings when in active growth.

Potting: Repot only when really necessary, as this orchid does not like to be disturbed and repotting can delay flowering for some time.

After flowering: Allow a cool rest period during the winter when the plant has stopped growing, but continue to water about every three weeks.

Colmanara Wildcat

This member of the *Odontoglossum* family makes a successful pot plant for a centrally heated home. It usually flowers in the spring or early summer and the blooms often remain in good condition for more than two months. There are many different varieties of Wildcat, with colors varying from ruby red to yellow, with brown markings.

Other *Colmanara* hybrids to consider: Jungle Monarch.

INDOOR CARE
Temperature: It grows best in daytime temperatures up to a maximum of 68°F (20°C), with nights not below 55°F (13°C). Although fairly tolerant, it will struggle with temperatures above 77°F (25°C). Avoid placing it too close to a radiator or in a draft.

Light: An east-facing window is ideal, but protect it from direct sunlight.
Watering: Water the growing medium thoroughly from the top when it is almost dry and allow the plant to drain. Never let it dry out completely.
Humidity: The higher the temperature, the higher the humidity required. If you live in a dry climate, stand the plant on a moist gravel tray to create a microclimate and assist growth.
Feeding: Include orchid fertilizer in three out of four waterings.
Potting: This should usually be carried out every other year. Repot when you can see 2–3 in (5–8 cm) of new growth.
After flowering: When the flowers die, cut back the stems to about 1 in (3 cm). Continue the watering and feeding regime, reducing the frequency of watering as temperatures start to drop.

Cymbidium lowianum 'concolor'

This extremely elegant plant is much sought after. Its blooms are quite different in shape from modern hybrids and are gracefully displayed on arching spikes. It flowers annually in the winter or early spring.

INDOOR CARE

Temperature: It grows best in daytime temperatures around 60°F (16°C), but never above 64°F (18°C). Nighttime temperatures should be around 50°F (10°C). Avoid placing too close to a radiator or in a draft.

Light: It requires a light spot, but should not be in direct sunlight.

Watering: Water thoroughly from the top when the growing medium is almost dry and allow the plant to drain. If in doubt—DON'T.

Humidity: In a dry atmosphere, stand the pot on a moist gravel tray to help prevent the leaf-tips from browning.

Feeding: Include orchid fertilizer in three out of four waterings, except in midsummer when the plant is starting to produce its spikes.

Potting: *Cymbidium* love to be potbound. Repot in spring, after flowering and only when the pot has become completely full of roots, probably every two to three years.

After flowering: When flowering has finished and after any danger of frost has passed, put the plant outside in dappled shade, perhaps under a tree. Bring it back inside before the first frosts arrive, acclimatizing it gradually to its winter temperature.

Cymbidium Sarah Jean

The flowers of this orchid are delicate and pretty, making it an ideal plant for displaying in a hanging basket. It flowers during the winter and early spring.

INDOOR CARE

Temperature: *Cymbidium* Sarah Jean grows best in a daytime temperature around 60°F (16°C), with nights down to 50°F (10°C). Avoid placing too close to a radiator or in a draft.

Light: It requires a light spot, but should not be placed in direct sunlight.

Watering: Water the plant thoroughly from the top when the growing medium is almost dry and allow it to drain.

Humidity: Mist leaves occasionally in hot weather.

Feeding: Include orchid fertilizer in three out of four waterings, except in midsummer when the plant is starting to produce its spikes.

Potting: *Cymbidium* love to be potbound. Repot in spring, after flowering and only when the pot becomes completely full of roots, probably every two years.

After flowering: When flowering has finished and after any danger of a late spring frost, put your plant outside in dappled shade, perhaps under a tree. Bring it back inside before the first fall frosts arrive, acclimatizing it gradually to its winter temperature.

Cymbidium (Miniature)

These are some of the easiest orchids to grow in a cool environment. However, the name "miniature" is misleading. These plants reach, on average, 18 in (45 cm) tall and produce 2 in (5 cm) flowers. Each spike can carry more than 10 blooms that may last up to three months on the plant. Varieties flower annually from late fall to early spring.

Varieties of *Cymbidium* to consider: Aviemore, Castle of Mey, King's Loch, Ming, Showgirl, Little Big Horn and many more.

INDOOR CARE

Temperature: It grows best in a daytime temperature around 60°F (16°C), with nights of 50°F (10°C). Avoid placing close to a radiator or in a draft.

Light: The plant requires a light spot, but it should not be in direct sunlight.

Watering: Water the plant thoroughly from the top when the growing medium is almost dry and allow it to drain.

Humidity: In a dry atmosphere, stand the pot on a moist gravel tray to help prevent the leaf-tips from browning.

Feeding: Include orchid fertilizer in three out of four waterings, except in midsummer when the plant is starting to produce its spikes.

Potting: *Cymbidium* love to be potbound. Repot after flowering, in the spring and only when the pot has become completely full of roots, probably every two years.

After flowering: When flowering has finished and any danger of late spring frost has passed, put your plant outside in dappled shade, perhaps under a tree. Bring it back inside before the first fall frosts arrive, acclimatizing it gradually to its winter temperature.

Below and right: Varieties of miniature *Cymbidium*—King's Loch and Ming 'Pagoda.'

Cymbidium (Miniature) continued

Below: A cheerful *Cymbidium* Aviemore 'December Orange.' For care instructions, see the profile on page 64.

Cymbidium (Standard)

These are some of the easiest groups of orchids to grow in a cool environment. The "standard" *Cymbidium* can grow into substantial plants—up to 3 ft (1 m) tall, with flowers over 4 in (10 cm) wide. Each spike can carry more than 10 blooms that may last up to three months. Young plants may have fewer blooms per stem. The plants usually flower during late winter to early spring. They come in a wide range of colors.

Other varieties of standard *Cymbidium* to consider: Christmas Joy, Dingwall, Sparkle, Pontac, Red Beauty and many more.

INDOOR CARE

Temperature: These *Cymbidium* grow best in a daytime temperature around 60°F (16°C), with nights down to 50°F (10°C). Avoid placing too close to a radiator or in a draft.

Light: Place in a light spot, but not in direct sunlight, as this will bleach out the flowers.

Watering: Water the plant thoroughly from the top when the growing medium is almost dry and allow it to drain.

Humidity: In a dry atmosphere, stand the pot on a moist gravel tray to help prevent the leaf-tips from browning.

Feeding: Include orchid fertilizer in three out of four waterings, except in midsummer when the plant is starting to produce its spikes.

Potting: *Cymbidium* love to be potbound. Repot in spring, after flowering, and only when the pot has become completely full of roots, probably every two to three years.

After flowering: When any danger of late spring frost has passed, put outside in dappled shade, perhaps under a tree. Bring it back inside before the first fall frosts arrive, acclimatizing it gradually to its winter temperature.

Below: *Cymbidium* Red Beauty is a modern classic, having large flowers with a prominent lip.

Above: *Cymbidium* Christmas Joy. For care instructions,
see the profile on page 67.

Above: *Cymbidium* Sparkle 'Ruby Lips.' For care instructions, see the profile on page 67.

Above: *Cymbidium* Dingwall. For care instructions,
see the profile on page 67.

Cymbidium tracyanum

The dramatic flowers of this orchid are quite different in shape from modern hybrids and are produced on long, arching stems. It flowers annually during the fall or winter.

INDOOR CARE

Temperature: It grows best in a daytime temperature around 60°F (16°C), with nights down to 50°F (10°C). Avoid placing it too close to a radiator or in a draft.

Light: The plant requires a light spot, but should not be in direct sunlight.

Watering: Water the plant thoroughly from the top when the growing medium is almost dry and allow it to drain.

Humidity: In a dry atmosphere, stand the pot on a moist gravel tray to help prevent the leaf-tips from browning.

Feeding: Include orchid fertilizer in three out of four waterings, except for a four-week period in midsummer when the plant is starting to produce its spikes.

Potting: *Cymbidium* love to be potbound. Repot in the spring and only when the pot has become completely full of roots, probably every two to three years.

After flowering: When the danger of frost has passed, put your plant outside in dappled shade. Bring it back inside when the plant starts to flower or before the first frosts arrive, acclimatizing it gradually to its winter temperature.

Dactylorhiza maculata

Commonly known as the Spotted Heath Orchid, this enchanting hardy orchid is widespread throughout Europe and can be grown as a perennial garden plant. In the fall, plant the tubers 2 in (5 cm) deep. In spring, the flower spikes are densely covered in small pinkish-purple flowers. Given protection from severe frosts, it can be left in the ground all year. In the right conditions it can multiply freely into large clumps.

TIP Happiest in a neutral or slightly acid soil with some added peat or leaf mold.

INDOOR CARE

Temperature: Where winters are severe, the plant can be grown in pots in an alpine house. It prefers temperatures below 64°F (18°C), with nights below 50°F (10°C).

Light: Prefers good light.

Watering: Keep moist, but not wet, all year.

Feeding: Benefits from a quarter-strength liquid feed every three weeks during leaf production. Stop when flower spikes appear.

Potting: Repot every year in the summer, after flowering. Use an open, loam-based growing medium with added grit. Remove the tubers and twist off the new from the old. Replant in a large pot at least 15 in (40 cm) deep. Place the tubers just below the surface and cover with 1 in (3 cm) of grit.

After flowering: The leaves will eventually die and the plant will rest until spring.

Dendrobium Emma 'White'

Commonly called Singapore Orchid, this popular hybrid makes a lovely houseplant. Its pretty white flowers are often used by florists for special occasions, particularly weddings.

Other *Dendrobium* hybrids to consider: Chiengmai 'Pink', Emma 'Pink,' Fantasy Land, Siam and many more.

INDOOR CARE

Temperature: The plant grows best in daytime temperatures above 68°F (20°C), with nights of about 60°F (16°C). It enjoys an airy position. Avoid placing too close to a radiator or in a draft.

Light: It needs bright, filtered light throughout the year.

Watering: Water freely while the plant is growing. Water from the top and allow it to drain thoroughly. Water is also absorbed from the atmosphere by the aerial roots outside the pot. Reduce watering during the fall and winter.

Humidity: If the atmosphere is dry, stand the plant on a moist gravel tray to create a microclimate and assist growth. Gently misting the plants early in the morning is also helpful.

Feeding: Include orchid fertilizer in three out of four waterings, from spring through fall.

Potting: Repot every two to three years when not in flower and ideally when you can see about 2 in (5 cm) of new growth. It prefers a small pot, just large enough for its roots. Use a growing medium that includes bark.

After flowering: Remove the dried-up flowers. Reduce the frequency of watering as temperatures start to drop, allowing the plant to rest.

Dendrobium kingianum

A variable species native to Australia, it has cane-like stems that produce sprays of long-lasting flowers in white, pink, purple or mauve. It flowers from late winter to early spring, often producing small plantlets (keikis) along the stems (*see page 40*). If cared for properly, it can grow into a large specimen plant.

INDOOR CARE

Temperature: This tolerant plant grows best in daytime temperatures of around 64°F (18°C), with nights not below 53°F (12°C). It loves an airy position. Avoid placing it too close to a radiator or in a draft. A cooler period (around 46°F (8°C)) for three to four weeks in the winter encourages flowering.

Light: It needs bright, filtered light throughout the year.

Watering: Water freely while the plant is growing in spring and summer. Reduce the frequency of watering as temperatures drop; about every three weeks in the winter. Water from the top and allow it to drain thoroughly. Mist weekly in the summer. Water is also absorbed from the atmosphere by the aerial roots outside the pot.

Humidity: If you live in a dry atmosphere, stand the plant on a moist gravel tray to create a microclimate and assist growth. Gently misting the plants early in the morning is also helpful.

Feeding: Include orchid fertilizer in three out of four waterings from spring through fall.

Potting: Repot every two to three years when not in flower and ideally when you can see about 2 in (5 cm) of new growth. Use a growing medium with a high bark content.

After flowering: Remove the flowers when they die.

Dendrobium nobile

This widely grown orchid has cane-like stems that produce several flower spikes of long-lasting, waxy, fragrant blooms. These are mostly white with lilac-pink streaks, and have a maroon patch at the center.

INDOOR CARE

Temperature: It grows best in daytime temperatures up to 68°F (20°C), with nights not below 55°F (13°C). The plant needs a cool period of about 46°F (8°C) during the winter for about three months to produce good flowers. It loves an airy position, but avoid drafts. Don't place it near a radiator.

Light: Provide it with bright, filtered light throughout the year.

Watering: Water freely while the plant is growing in the spring and summer. Water from the top and allow it to drain thoroughly. Stop watering the plant during its cool period. Water is also absorbed from the atmosphere by the aerial roots outside the pot.

Humidity: If you live in a dry atmosphere, stand the plant on a moist gravel tray to create a microclimate and assist growth. A gentle misting early in the morning during the summer is also useful when the air is really dry.

Feeding: Benefits from regular feeding. Include orchid fertilizer in three out of four waterings during spring and summer.

Potting: Repot every two to three years when not in flower and ideally when you can see about 2 in (5 cm) of new growth. It prefers a small pot. Use an orchid mix that includes medium-grade bark.

After flowering: Remove dried-up flowers. Position the plant in a light, airy spot during the cool period.

Dendrobium Sailor Boy

Modern breeding of *Dendrobium nobile* has produced many hybrids that have masses of flowers in a range of colors. One example is this eye-catching white orchid. It flowers midwinter to early summer.

Other hybrids to consider: Yamamoto, Upin Red 'Mini,' New Comet 'Red Queen,' Himezakura 'Sanock,' Comet King 'Akatsuki,' Milky Road, Stardust 'Chyomi,' Stardust 'Firebird,' and Spring Dream 'Kumiko.'

INDOOR CARE

Temperature: The plant grows best in daytime temperatures up to 68°F (20°C), with nights not below 55°F (13°C) during the summer months. It needs a cool period of around 46°F (8°C) during the winter for about three months to produce good flowers. Avoid placing too close to a radiator or in a draft.

Light: It requires bright, filtered light throughout the year.

Watering: Water freely while the plant is growing in the spring and summer. Water from the top and allow it to drain thoroughly. Stop watering during its cool period. Water is also absorbed from the atmosphere by the aerial roots outside the pot.

Humidity: If you live in a dry atmosphere, stand the plant on a moist gravel tray to create a microclimate and assist growth. During the summer, gently misting the plants early in the morning helps to increase humidity if the air is very dry.

Feeding: Include orchid fertilizer in three out of four waterings in spring and summer.

Potting: Repot every two to three years when not in flower and when you can see about 2 in (5 cm) of new growth. It prefers a small pot. Use a growing medium that includes bark.

After flowering: Remove dried-up flowers. Place the plant in a light, airy spot during its cool period.

Left: The abundant, vivid blooms of *Dendrobium* Stardust are massed around each stem. For care instructions, see the profile above for *Dendrobium* Sailor Boy.

Dendrobium Thongchai Gold

This orchid makes an excellent house plant, as it is very tolerant. The cane-like stems produce flower spikes of up to 20 blooms that can last for two months.

INDOOR CARE

Temperature: It grows best in daytime temperatures above 68°F (20°C), with nights not below 60°F (16°C). It enjoys an airy position, but avoid placing it too close to a radiator or in a draft.

Light: It needs bright, filtered light throughout the year.

Watering: Water freely while it is growing, which could be for most of the year. Water the plant from the top and allow it to drain thoroughly. Water is also absorbed from the atmosphere by the aerial roots outside the pot. Reduce watering during the fall and winter, when temperatures drop, and allow the plant to rest.

Humidity: If you live in a dry atmosphere, stand the plant on a moist gravel tray to create a microclimate and assist growth. Gently misting the plants early in the morning also helps if the air is very dry.

> **TIP** Although this orchid appreciates good humidity, too much moisture encourages little plantlets (keikis) to form along the canes, instead of flowers (*see page 40*).

Feeding: Include orchid fertilizer in three out of four waterings, during the spring and summer.

Potting: Repot every two to three years when not in flower and ideally when you can see about 2 in (5 cm) of new growth. Use a medium-grade bark orchid mix. It prefers a small pot.

After flowering: When the flowers die, cut the stem back, leaving about 1 in (3 cm). Continue the watering and feeding regime all year.

Doritaenopsis Heverlee

A relative of the *Phalaenopsis*, moth orchid, *Doritaenopsis* makes an ideal pot plant for a centrally heated home. Its flowers may look delicate, but they are quite robust, often remaining in good condition for more than three months. This modern hybrid carries seven or more flowers on each stem. It may produce flower spikes in any season and usually reflowers within the year.

Other *Doritaenopsis* hybrids to consider: there are hundreds of varieties to choose from.

INDOOR CARE

Temperature: The plant grows best in daytime temperatures above 68°F (20°C), with nights not below 60°F (16°C). Avoid placing it too close to a radiator or in a draft.

Light: Indirect sunlight is ideal.

Watering: Water thoroughly from the top when the growing medium is almost dry and allow to drain. Keep the center of the plant dry. Water is also absorbed from the atmosphere by the aerial roots outside the pot.

Humidity: The higher the temperature, the higher the humidity required. If the air is dry, a gentle misting early in the morning can be useful, as is placing the plant on a humidity tray.

Feeding: Include orchid fertilizer in three out of four waterings.

Potting: This is best done every other year during the spring, when the plant is not in flower.

After flowering: When the flowers die, cut the stem back to about 10 in (25 cm). Continue the watering and feeding regime, and a new flower spike may be produced from a node (*see page 40*).

If the stem dies back, cut it down to about 1 in (3 cm). Continue the watering and feeding regime all year. A new spike will appear from the base of the plant in about seven to 10 months.

> **TIP** Should a healthy plant fail to produce a flower spike in a reasonable time (10 months), reduce the temperature by 10°F (5°C) for four weeks to encourage flowering.

Doritis pulcherrima

This plant is a good choice for a centrally heated home. Each flower stem carries several flowers that open successively and often last for over three months. Mature plants usually produce more than one flowering stem, which appear from late summer to early winter.

INDOOR CARE

Temperature: *Doritis pulcherrima* grows best in daytime temperatures above 68°F (20°C), with nights not below 60°F (16°C). Avoid placing too close to a radiator or in a draft.
Light: Partial shade is ideal.
Watering: Water the plant thoroughly from the top when the growing medium is almost dry and allow it to drain. Keep the center of the plant dry. Water is also absorbed from the atmosphere by the aerial roots outside the pot.
Humidity: The higher the temperature, the higher the humidity required. A gentle misting early in the morning is useful when the air is dry.
Feeding: Include orchid fertilizer in three out of four waterings.
Potting: This should usually be done every other year in late spring, when the plant is not in flower.
After flowering: When the flowers die, cut the stem back to about 1 in (3 cm). Continue the watering and feeding regime all year.

> **TIP** If a healthy plant fails to produce a flower spike in a reasonable time (10 months), reduce the temperature by 10°F (5°C) for four weeks to encourage flowering.

Encyclia cochleata

When small, this plant happily sits on a windowsill, but after several years of good growing, it may well become too large for that position. Each flower stem carries several blooms that open successively, generally two to three at a time, providing a long flowering period. A mature plant may flower all year round. Its common names include Clamshell or Cockle orchid and Octopussy.

INDOOR CARE

Temperature: *Encyclia cochleata* prefers daytime temperatures around 68°F (20°C), with nights not below 55°F (13°C). Avoid placing too close to a radiator or in a draft.

Light: Partial shade is ideal.

Watering: Water thoroughly from the top when the growing medium is almost dry and allow it to drain.

Humidity: The higher the temperature, the higher the humidity required. A gentle misting early in the morning is useful if the air is dry.

Feeding: Include orchid fertilizer in three out of four waterings.

Potting: This is best done every other year in late spring, when the plant is not in flower.

After flowering: When the flowers die, cut the stem back to about 1 in (3 cm). Continue the watering and feeding regime all year.

Encyclia vitellina

This orchid produces elegantly shaped, long-lasting blooms of a stunning orange. It usually flowers in the fall or early spring. The leaves have a blue/gray bloom, which contrasts well with the showy flowers.

INDOOR CARE

Temperature: *Encyclia vitellina* grows best in daytime temperatures above 68°F (20°C), with nights not below 60°F (16°C). Avoid placing too close to a radiator or in a draft.

Light: Indirect sunlight is ideal.

Watering: Water thoroughly from the top when the growing medium is almost dry and allow to drain.

Humidity: The higher the temperature, the higher the humidity required. A gentle misting early in the morning can be useful if the air is dry.

Feeding: Include orchid fertilizer in three out of four waterings.

Potting: This is usually carried out every other year in late spring, when the plant is not in flower.

After flowering: When the flowers die, cut the stem back to about 1 in (3 cm). Continue the watering and feeding regime all year.

Epicattleya Fire Bird

This member of the *Cattleya* family is a good choice for a colorful pot plant. It flowers in the spring, when six or seven striking flowers are massed at the end of each stem. Each flower lasts for three to four weeks on the plant, but because they bloom successively, the plant gives a flowering period of over two months. Epiphytic roots appear above the growing medium.

Other *Epicattleya* to consider: Purple Glory, Rene.

INDOOR CARE

Temperature: *Epicattleya* Fire Bird grows best in daytime temperatures above 68°F (20°C), but enjoys cooler nights, down to 55°F (13°C). Avoid placing too close to a radiator or in a draft.

Light: It thrives on good light, but requires protection from full midday sun. It can be grown on an east- or west-facing window.

Watering: Water the plant frequently when growing, but allow it to dry out a little between waterings. Water thoroughly from the top and allow it to drain. Reduce frequency as temperatures drop and light levels decrease. During the winter a drying-out period of two to three months is beneficial, when the plant should be watered about every six weeks. Gradually increase watering in the spring to encourage new growth.

Humidity: The higher the temperature, the higher the humidity required. In a dry atmosphere, stand the plant on a moist gravel tray to create a microclimate and assist growth.

 TIP This plant loves an airy atmosphere.

Feeding: Include orchid fertilizer in three out of four waterings.

Potting: Repot every two to three years in spring when new growth appears. Use a medium-coarse bark orchid mix.

After flowering: Remove dead flowers and sheaths.

Epidendrum ibaguense 'Ballerina Yellow'

The many small flowers of this plant are clustered together for impact, and can last for several weeks. The orchid usually has three or more stems. Flowering takes place from winter to early spring.

Other *Epidendrum ibaguense* varieties to consider: 'Ballerina Purple,' 'Ballerina Snow' (white), 'Ballerina Tropical' (yellow turning to orange) and 'Ballerina Fireball' (reddish-orange).

INDOOR CARE

Temperature: Although in the intermediate temperature-growing category, this plant is, in fact, extremely tolerant, surviving temperatures as high as 86°F (30°C) and as low as 54°F (12°C). Avoid placing it too close to a radiator or in a draft.

Light: An east- or west-facing window is ideal. It likes good light, but should not be in direct sunlight.

Watering: Water thoroughly from the top when the growing medium is almost dry and allow it to drain. Never let the plant sit in water.

Humidity: If you live in a dry atmosphere, stand the plant on a moist gravel tray to create a microclimate and assist growth. Gently mist the leaves early in the morning if the air is dry.

Feeding: Include orchid fertilizer in three out of four waterings.

Potting: . Repot every other year when you can see 2–3 in (5–8 cm) of new growth.

After flowering: When the flowers die, remove the flower heads. Continue the watering and feeding regime all year.

> **TIP** Deadheading (removing the dead flowers) encourages new flowering.

Epiphronitis Veitchii

This orchid features clusters of brilliant orange-red and yellow flowers in the spring. If you live in a warm climate, the plant can be put outside in a sheltered spot during the summer.

INDOOR CARE

Temperature: *Epiphronitis* Veitchii prefers daytime temperatures of 68°F (20°C), with nights around 55°F (13°C). Avoid placing it too close to a radiator or in a draft. This plant needs a cooler position in the winter with daytime temperatures between 53 and 59°F (12 and 15°C).

Light: An east- or west-facing window is ideal. It enjoys good light, almost full sun.

Watering: If the plant is in a warm room, water it about once a week from the top when the growing medium is almost dry and allow it to drain. If it is in a cooler room, it will need watering less often. Never let the plant sit in water.

Humidity: If you live in a dry climate, stand the plant on a moist gravel tray to create a microclimate and assist growth.

Feeding: Include orchid fertilizer in three out of four waterings.

Potting: Repot every other year when you can see 2–3 in (5–8 cm) of new growth.

After flowering: After flowering has finished, cut the stems back to about 2 in (5 cm). Continue the watering and feeding regime all year.

Laelia anceps

This is a classic corsage orchid with fragrant, showy flowers, produced on tall flower stems. It is the parent of many shorter hybrids available today.

Related hybrids to consider: *Laeliocattleya* 'Puppy Love,' *Lc.* 'Angel Love,' *Lc.* 'Sylvan Sprite.'

INDOOR CARE

Temperature: *Laelia anceps* prefers minimum temperatures of around 55°F (13°C), but it is extremely tolerant and can survive daytime heat of up to 100°F (38°C), provided it has good humidity. It enjoys an airy position, but avoid positioning it too close to a radiator or in a draft.

Light: It prefers good light, but needs protection from direct sunlight.

Watering: Water freely while the plant is growing, but let the roots dry out between waterings. Water from the top and allow the plant to drain thoroughly. Reduce frequency of watering in the winter to about once a month. Water is also absorbed from the atmosphere by the aerial roots outside the pot.

Humidity: In a dry atmosphere, stand the pot on a moist gravel tray to help raise humidity. Gently mist the leaves early in the morning if temperatures are above 71°F (22°C).

Feeding: Benefits from regular feeding. Include orchid fertilizer in three out of four waterings.

Potting: Repot only when really necessary. This is usually carried out directly after flowering using a medium-coarse bark. When sufficiently large, the plant can be divided, leaving three pseudobulbs on each piece. The plant may require staking with a cane or two to keep it stable, particularly when mature.

After flowering: When the flowers die, cut the stem back to about 1 in (3 cm). Continue the watering and feeding regime all year, but reduce the frequency as temperatures begin to fall.

Laelia gouldiana

This orchid's flowers are produced on tall stems, so choose your plant's position carefully. It will enjoy a warm, bright situation. With good cultivation, this plant will grow into a large, freely branching specimen.

INDOOR CARE

Temperature: It prefers minimum temperatures of 55°F (13°C), but it can cope with daytime heat of up to 100°F (38°C), provided it has good humidity. It enjoys an airy position, but avoid placing it too close to a radiator or in a draft.

Light: It needs good light, but should be protected from direct sunlight.

Watering: Water thoroughly while growing, but allow the roots to dry out between waterings. Water from the top and allow the plant to drain. Reduce frequency to about once a month in the winter. Water is also absorbed from the atmosphere by the aerial roots outside the pot.

Humidity: In a dry atmosphere, stand the pot on a moist gravel tray to help raise humidity. Gently mist the leaves early in the morning if temperatures are above 71°F (22°C).

Feeding: Include orchid fertilizer in three out of four waterings.

Potting: Repotting should usually be carried out directly after flowering, using a medium-coarse bark. When the plant is large enough, it can be divided, leaving three pseudobulbs on each piece. When mature, it may need to be staked with a cane or two to keep it stable.

After flowering: When the flowers die, cut the stem back to about 1 in (3 cm). Continue the watering and feeding regime all year, but reduce the frequency as temperatures begin to fall.

Laelia purpurata

The national flower of Brazil, this orchid produces showy flowers in white or pink, and is suitable for a warm and bright position. It has been used on many occasions to produce stunning hybrids in a range of colors.

Others to consider: with over 13,000 registered descendants, there is an enormous choice.

INDOOR CARE

Temperature: It prefers minimum temperatures of around 60°F (16°C), but can tolerate summer heat of up to 100°F (38°C), provided it has good humidity. It enjoys an airy position, but avoid positioning too close to a radiator or in a draft.

Light: It thrives in good light, but protect it from full, midday sun. It can be grown in an east- or west-facing window, or even a lightly shaded south-facing window.

Watering: Water thoroughly while the plant is growing, but allow the roots to dry out between waterings. Water from the top of the growing medium and allow it to drain thoroughly. Reduce frequency as the temperature drops and light levels fall. By the time winter arrives, water about once a month for a period of three to four months. Gradually increase watering in the spring to encourage new growth. Water is also absorbed from the atmosphere by the aerial roots outside the pot.

> **TIP** If the leaves and pseudobulbs are wrinkled, your plant needs more water.

Humidity: The higher the temperature, the higher the humidity required. In a dry atmosphere, stand the plant on a moist gravel tray to create a microclimate and raise humidity. Gently mist the leaves early in the morning if temperatures are above 71°F (22°C).

Feeding: Benefits from regular feeding. Include orchid fertilizer in three out of four waterings.

Potting: Repot every two to three years after flowering, using medium-coarse bark. Large plants may require staking with a small cane to keep them stable.

After flowering: When the blooms die, cut the flower stem back to about 1 in (3 cm). Continue the watering and feeding regime all year, but reduce the frequency as temperatures start to drop.

Laeliocattleya Love Knot

    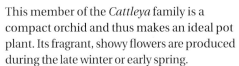

This member of the *Cattleya* family is a compact orchid and thus makes an ideal pot plant. Its fragrant, showy flowers are produced during the late winter or early spring.

Others to consider: there are many orchids in this family, including Mini Purple, Gold Digger and Blue Indigo.

INDOOR CARE

Temperature: It prefers minimum temperatures of around 60°F (16°C), but can tolerate summer heat of up to 100°F (38°C) provided it has good humidity. It enjoys an airy position, but avoid positioning too close to a radiator or in a draft.

Light: It thrives in good light, but needs protection from full, midday sun. It can be grown in an east- or west-facing window, or even a lightly shaded south-facing window.

Watering: Water thoroughly while the plant is growing, but allow the roots to dry out between waterings. Water the top of the growing medium and let it drain thoroughly.

Reduce frequency as temperatures and light levels drop. By the time winter arrives, the plant should be watered about once a month for a period of about three months. Gradually increase watering in the spring to encourage new growth. Water is also absorbed from the atmosphere by the aerial roots outside the pot.

Humidity: The higher the temperature, the more humidity required. In a dry atmosphere, stand the plant on a moist gravel tray to create a microclimate and raise humidity. Gently mist the leaves early in the morning if temperatures are above 71°F (22°C).

Feeding: Benefits from regular feeding. Include orchid fertilizer in three out of four waterings.

Potting: This is usually carried out every two to three years after flowering, using medium-coarse bark. Some plants may require staking with a small cane to keep them stable.

After flowering: When the blooms die, cut the flower stem back to about 1 in (3 cm). Continue the watering and feeding regime all year, but reduce the frequency as temperatures start to drop.

Ludisia discolor

Commonly known as the Jewel orchid, this is one of a small group grown for their beautiful leaves, rather than their flowers. As it grows, the plant's fleshy stems spread outwards. In the winter, small ivory blooms appear clustered around tall flower stalks. Flowering lasts about two weeks.

INDOOR CARE

Temperature: *Ludisia discolor* prefers minimum nighttime temperatures of around 60°F (16°C), but is tolerant as far as daytime temperatures are concerned. It enjoys an airy position, but avoid placing it too close to a radiator or in a draft.

Light: Grow in a north-facing window. It dislikes being in direct sunlight, which would bleach out the colorful leaves.

Watering: Water the top of the growing medium and drain thoroughly. Allow it to nearly dry out before watering again.

Humidity: The higher the temperature, the more humidity required. In a dry atmosphere, stand the plant on a moist gravel tray to create a microclimate and raise humidity. Don't be tempted to mist it; avoid wetting the leaves.

Feeding: Include orchid fertilizer in three out of four waterings.

Potting: Repot every two years after flowering. A shallow, wide pot (pan) is ideal. Use medium-coarse bark mixed with a little sphagnum moss.

> **TIP** As the stems outgrow the pot, they occasionally break off. Plant the "cutting" in a small pot of sphagnum moss and water it thoroughly. Leave in a shady, warm place and roots should start to develop in about six weeks.

After flowering: When the blooms die, cut the flower stem back. Continue the watering and feeding regime all year.

Masdevallia Ted Khoe

In the wild, most *Masdevallia* need cool and airy, but humid conditions—which are not easy to recreate in our homes. Hybrids have been bred to be less demanding and prefer warmer surroundings. This orchid usually flowers in the late winter to early spring, producing stunning blooms of a vivid color. Other hybrids flower throughout the summer.

Other hybrids to consider: Confetti, Copper Angel, Rose-Mary.

INDOOR CARE

Temperature: The plant grows best in daytime temperatures of around 68°F (20°C), with nights around 55°F (13°C). It loves an airy position, but avoid placing it too close to a radiator or in a draft.

Light: Grow in an east- or west-facing window. It prefers partial shade.

Watering: Water from the top of the growing medium and drain thoroughly. Allow the growing medium to nearly dry out before watering again, but never let it dry out completely.

Humidity: In a dry atmosphere, stand the plant on a moist gravel tray to create a microclimate and raise humidity. Gently mist the leaves in the morning if temperatures rise above 71°F (22°C).

> **TIP** Good air movement is the key to preventing fungal infections.

Feeding: Include orchid fertilizer in three out of four waterings.

Potting: Repot every one to two years in winter or early spring, after flowering. Use a sphagnum moss and perlite mix, or a fine-grade orchid potting mix. Keep humidity levels up, but reduce watering until new roots form. It prefers a small pot.

After flowering: When the blooms die, cut the flower stem back to tidy the plant. Continue the watering and feeding regime all year.

Miltonia spectabilis 'Moreliana'

A native of Brazil, *Miltonia spectabilis* is easier to grow as a houseplant than its Colombian cousin, *Miltoniopsis*. Both are commonly called the Pansy orchid because of their resemblance to the garden plant. This choice orchid produces satiny blooms in shades of plum and deep pink, with a spicy fragrance. The more common varieties are found in shades of creamy-white with a hint of rose. Flowering usually occurs in the late summer or early fall. A large plant makes a wonderful display.

INDOOR CARE

Temperature: The plant prefers daytime temperatures of 68°F (20°C), with nights not below 55°F (13°C). Avoid placing it too close to a radiator or in a draft.

Light: An east- or west-facing window is fine. Partial shade is good.

Watering: Water the growing medium thoroughly from the top when it is almost dry and allow it to drain. Never let it dry out completely. Water less frequently as temperatures start to fall.

Humidity: If you live in a dry climate, stand the plant on a moist gravel tray to create a microclimate and assist growth. If grown on a raft, spray the leaves in the early morning when temperatures are above 71°F (22°C). Take care not to splash the flowers.

> **TIP** Avoid extreme fluctuations in humidity and watering, as this can cause a corrugated effect on the plant's leaves.

Feeding: Include half-strength orchid fertilizer in three out of four waterings.

Potting: This should usually be carried out every two to three years in spring, but not when in flower. Use a free-draining medium.

After flowering: When the blooms die, cut the flower stem back to about 1 in (3 cm). Continue the watering and feeding regime all year.

Miltonidium Hawaiian Sunset

This orchid from the *Odontoglossum* family produces approximately 20 spikes of long-lasting flowers in deep pink and gold. Aerial roots can sometimes be seen outside the pot. Depending on age, plants may have two or more stems.

Other *Miltonidium* to consider: Avalon Bay, Rosy Sunset, Summer Fantasy.

INDOOR CARE

Temperature: This orchid prefers daytime temperatures of around 77°F (25°C), with nights not below 60°F (16°C). Avoid placing it too close to a radiator or in a draft.

Light: An east- or west-facing window is ideal. It prefers partial shade.

Watering: Water the growing medium thoroughly from the top when it is almost dry and allow it to drain. Never let it dry out completely.

Humidity: The higher the temperature, the higher the humidity required. If you live in a dry climate, stand the plant on a moist gravel tray to create a microclimate and assist growth.

Feeding: Include half-strength orchid fertilizer in three out of four waterings.

Potting: This should be usually carried out every other year in early fall, but not when in flower.

After flowering: When the blooms die, cut the flower stem back to about 1 in (3 cm). Continue the watering and feeding regime all year, but reduce the frequency of watering as temperatures start to cool down.

Above: *Miltonidium* Bartley Schwartz is a compact grower with good-sized blooms. It is an ideal choice for a potplant, as it is both fragrant and tolerant. For care instructions, see the profile for *Miltonidium* Hawaiian Sunset opposite.

Miltoniopsis Red Knight

This orchid produces spikes of long-lasting, scented flowers, resembling those of the garden pansy, which appear from late winter through to early summer. Sometimes aerial roots can be seen outside the pot. Depending on age, plants may have two or more stems.

Other Pansy orchids to consider: Emotion, Herralexandre, Jersey, Saint Helier.

INDOOR CARE

Temperature: It prefers daytime temperatures of around 59–68°F (15–20°C). with little fluctuation. Nighttime temperatures should not be below 55°F (13°C). Avoid placing the plant too close to a radiator or in a draft.

Light: An east- or west-facing window is fine. It prefers partial shade.

Watering: Water the plant freely while it is growing. Water the growing medium thoroughly from the top when it is almost dry and allow it to drain. Never let it dry out completely. Less water will be needed when the pseudobulbs mature. Reduce watering as temperatures start to fall. Avoid wetting the flowers as this could mark them.

Humidity: If you live in a dry climate, stand the plant on a moist gravel tray to create a microclimate and assist growth.

Feeding: Include half-strength orchid fertilizer in three out of four waterings.

Potting: Repot every two to three years in spring, but not when in flower.

After flowering: When the blooms die, cut the flower stem back to about 1 in (3 cm). Continue the watering and feeding regime all year.

> **TIP** Large fluctuations in humidity and watering can cause a corrugated effect on the leaves.

Above: Distinctive *Miltoniopsis* Charlesworthii x Seine. For care
instructions, see the profile for Red Knight opposite.

Above: The vibrant pink *Miltoniopsis* Emotion. For care
instructions, see the profile for Red Knight on page 96.

Neopabstopetalum Clarendon

When mature, this member of the *Zygopetalum* family will produce several spikes of wonderfully fragrant flowers. Patterning will vary from plant to plant, as they are seed-raised. Its peak flowering time is from the spring to early summer, but it may flower again later in the year.

Other *Neopabstopetalum* to consider: Adelaide, Angaston, Rymill Park, Wallaroo.

INDOOR CARE

Temperature: The plant grows best in daytime temperatures of around 62–77°F (17–25°C), with nights not below 50°F (10°C). For short periods, however, it can tolerate more extreme temperatures—days of up to 95°F (35°C), and much colder nights.

Light: It prefers partial shade. An east- or west-facing window is ideal.

Watering: Water the growing medium thoroughly from the top when it is almost dry and allow it to drain.

Humidity: The higher the temperature, the higher the humidity required. If you live in a dry atmosphere, standing the plant on a moist gravel tray will raise humidity.

> **TIP** Good air movement will help dry the leaves after watering. If the foliage remains damp, crown rot may attack at the base of the leaves.

Feeding: Include orchid fertilizer in three out of four waterings.

Potting: Repot every year in the spring or early summer. Choose a container not more than 1 in (2–3 cm) larger than its current one—this will allow sufficient space for only two new pseudobulbs to develop before next repotting. Use a well-aerated, free-draining orchid mix.

After flowering: Cut back the stems to about 1 in (3 cm). Continue the watering and feeding regime, reducing the frequency of watering as temperatures start to cool down.

> **TIP** If a healthy plant with a new pseudobulb is reluctant to flower, place it in a cooler room for a couple of weeks when new growth starts to emerge.

Odontoglossum Geyser Gold

The vast majority of the *Odontoglossum* family are not suitable as houseplants. Being extremely particular as to temperature and water quality, they are best left to enthusiasts. However, hybridists have produced two that can be grown successfully in the home: Geyser Gold and Violetta von Holm.

Geyser Gold produces spikes of flowers that often remain in good condition for over two months. It's an unusual variety in that it has no red pigment, resulting in clean yellow and white flowers. The plants may have one or more stems, depending on age.

INDOOR CARE

Temperature: This plant prefers daytime temperatures of 68°F (20°C), but can tolerate up to 79°F (26°C) for short periods, with nights not below 55°F (13°C). Avoid placing too close to a radiator or in a draft.

Light: A north- or west-facing window is ideal. The plant does not like direct sunlight.

Watering: Water the growing medium thoroughly from the top when it is almost dry and allow it to drain. Never let it dry out completely or sit in water.

Humidity: Shriveled pseudobulbs can be the sign of a dry atmosphere. Standing the plant on a moist gravel tray will raise humidity. Gently mist the leaves early in the morning if temperatures rise above 68°F (20°C).

Feeding: Include half-strength orchid fertilizer in three out of four waterings.

Potting: This should usually be carried out every other year in early fall, but not when in flower.

> **TIP** This variety has been selected because it can be grown successfully as a houseplant. Most *Odontoglossum* are not as tolerant.

After flowering: Cut the flower stem back to about 1 in (3 cm). Continue the watering and feeding regime, reducing watering as temperatures start to drop.

Above: *Odontoglossum* Violetta von Holm is a compact plant with erect spikes of very unusual flowers. This is one of the very few *Odontoglossum* that can be grown as a houseplant. For care instructions, see the profile for *Odontoglossum* Geyser Gold on page 100.

Oncidium Sharry Baby

This established pot plant produces fragrant spikes of chocolate-scented flowers that often last for more than two months. The flowers are purplish-maroon and pink with brown speckles. Aerial roots can be seen outside the pot. Depending on age, plants may have more than one stem.

INDOOR CARE

Temperature: *Oncidium* Sharry Baby prefers daytime temperatures of around 77°F (25°C), with nights not below 55°F (13°C). It can tolerate higher temperatures, provided that humidity and air movement are increased. Avoid placing it too close to a radiator or in a draft.

Light: It thrives on good light, but requires protection from full, midday sun. It can be grown in an east- or west-facing window, or even a lightly shaded south-facing window.

Watering: Water the growing medium thoroughly from the top when it is almost dry and allow it to drain. Never let the growing medium dry out completely.

Humidity: The plant does not need high humidity, but if you live in a dry climate, stand it on a moist gravel tray to raise humidity and assist growth.

Feeding: Include half-strength orchid fertilizer in three out of four waterings.

Potting: Repot every other year in the spring, but not when in flower. Use a medium-grade orchid growing mix or bark.

After flowering: When the blooms die, cut the flower stem back to about 1 in (3 cm). Continue the watering and feeding regime.

Oncidium Sweet Sugar

This proven pot plant, known as Dancing Ladies, is a good grower and ideal for centrally heated homes. It produces spikes of long-lasting flowers that often remain in good condition for over two months. It likes an airy spot to "dance" in. Sometimes aerial roots can be seen outside the pot. Plants may have one or more stems, depending on age.

INDOOR CARE

Temperature: It prefers daytime temperatures between 71 and 77°F (22 and 25°C), with nights around 60°F (16°C). It is unhappy with temperatures any lower than 55°F (13°C). It can tolerate higher temperatures as long as humidity and air movement are increased. Avoid placing too close to a radiator or in a draft.

Light: It thrives in good light, but protect from full, midday sun. Grow in an east- or west-facing window, or even a lightly shaded south-facing window.

Watering: Water the growing medium thoroughly from the top when it is almost dry and allow to drain. Never let the growing medium dry out completely.

Humidity: This orchid does not need high humidity. Most homes will be fine, but if you live in a dry climate, stand the plant on a moist gravel tray to raise humidity levels and assist growth.

Feeding: Include half-strength orchid fertilizer in three out of four waterings.

Potting: Repot every other year in the spring, but not when in flower. Use a medium-grade orchid growing mix or bark.

After flowering: When the blooms die, cut the flower stem back to about 1 in (3 cm). Continue the watering and feeding regime all year.

Oncidium Twinkle

This pretty plant produces as many as 20 or 30 small, sweet-scented flowers on its branching stems. Most plants will have several stems, giving a "frothy" effect. Each tiny bloom can last for up to a month and, as the spikes are produced in succession, it can remain in flower for more than two months. Colors range from white, through cream to soft red. It flowers from winter to early summer.

INDOOR CARE

Temperature: *Oncidium* Twinkle prefers daytime temperatures of around 68°F (20°C), with nights not below 55°F (13°C). Avoid placing too close to a radiator or in a draft.

Light: An east- or west-facing window is ideal. It likes good light, but not direct sunlight.

Watering: Water the growing medium thoroughly from the top and allow it to drain. Never let it dry out completely or sit in water.

Humidity: If you live in a dry atmosphere, standing the plant on a moist gravel tray will create a microclimate and assist growth.

Feeding: Include half-strength orchid fertilizer in three out of four waterings.

Potting: Repot every two years after flowering. It prefers a small pot (the exact size depends entirely on the size of the plant) and a medium-grade orchid growing mix or bark.

After flowering: When the blooms die, cut the flower stem back to about 1 in (3 cm). Continue the watering and feeding regime all year.

Above: *Oncidium* Twinkle can also be found in pretty pinks and red.

Osmoglossum pulchellum

This pretty plant produces fragrant spikes of white, long-lasting flowers, which are held the opposite way to most orchids—"lip up." Plants may have more than one stem, depending on age.

INDOOR CARE

Temperature: It prefers daytime temperatures of around 68°F (20°C), with nights not below 55°F (13°C). Avoid placing too close to a radiator or in a draft.

Light: A north- or west-facing window is ideal. It likes good indirect sunlight.

Watering: Water the growing medium thoroughly from the top when it is almost dry and allow it to drain. Never let it dry out completely or sit in water.

Humidity: If you live in a dry climate, stand the plant on a moist gravel tray to help raise humidity levels and assist growth.

Feeding: Include half-strength orchid fertilizer in three out of four waterings.

Potting: This should usually be carried out every other year in early fall, but not when in flower.

After flowering: When the blooms die, cut the flower stem back to about 1 in (3 cm). Continue the watering and feeding regime all year.

Paphiopedilum bellatulum

These exotic plants easily adapt to normal household temperatures. Their distinctive "lip" looks like a slipper and explains why they are known as Slipper orchids or Lady's Slipper. They produce plump, spotted blooms in many colors, which can last for up to three months, and have mottled leaves.

INDOOR CARE

Temperature: This orchid grows best in daytime temperatures of around 77°F (25°C), with nights not below 64°F (18°C). Avoid placing too close to a radiator or in a draft.

Light: Partial shade is ideal. It will need protection from hot, midday sun.

Watering: Water thoroughly from the top and allow the growing medium to drain. Try to keep it moist, but not too wet. Take care that water does not lodge between the leaves or in the center.

> **TIP** If water does lodge between the leaves or in the center, dab lightly with some twisted tissue to soak up the excess.

Humidity: It likes an airy atmosphere. The higher the temperature, the higher the humidity required.

Feeding: Include half-strength orchid fertilizer in three out of four waterings.

Potting: Repot every year after flowering. This plant likes a small pot, and a bark and sphagnum mix. When the plant has grown large enough, it can be divided.

After flowering: When the flowers die, cut the stem back to about 1 in (3 cm). Continue the watering and feeding regime all year.

Paphiopedilum delenatii x moquettianum

The crossing of these two species has produced handsome Slipper orchids in whites, cream, and pale pinks, with marbled foliage. They make good pot plants, usually producing two or three flowers on each stem, which bloom in succession.

INDOOR CARE

Temperature: This plant prefers daytime temperatures above 70–82°F (21–28°C), with nights not below 64°F (18°C). Avoid placing too close to a radiator or in a draft.

Light: Indirect sunlight is ideal. Provide shade if growing in a conservatory.

Watering: Water thoroughly from the top when the growing medium is almost dry and allow it to drain. Try to keep the growing medium just moist, but not wet. Take care that water does not lodge between the leaves or in the center of the plant.

> **TIP** If water does lodge between the leaves or in the center of the plant, dab lightly with some twisted tissue to soak up the excess.

Humidity: The higher the temperature, the higher the humidity required.

Feeding: Include half-strength orchid fertilizer in three out of four waterings.

Potting: This should usually be carried out every year in late spring, when not in flower. It likes a small pot, and a bark and sphagnum mix.

After flowering: When the flowers die, cut the stem back to about 1 in (3 cm). Continue the watering and feeding regime all year.

Paphiopedilum Hellas

This is a variety with plain green leaves, which generally prefer a cooler temperature than the mottled-leafed types of Slipper orchid. It produces a single, glossy flower on each stem.

There are hundreds of other cool-growing Slipper orchids to consider: these include Coral Sea, Dusky Maiden, Greensleeves, Winston Churchill.

INDOOR CARE

Temperature: The plant grows best in daytime temperatures of 64°F (18°C), with nights not below 50°F (10°C). Avoid placing too close to a radiator or in a draft.

Light: Partial shade is ideal.

Watering: Water thoroughly from the top and allow it to drain. Try to keep the growing medium moist, but not wet. Take care that water does not lodge between the leaves or in the center.

> **TIP** If water does lodge between the leaves or in the center, just dab lightly with some twisted tissue to soak up the excess.

Humidity: The higher the temperature, the higher the humidity required.

Feeding: Include half-strength orchid fertilizer in three out of four waterings.

Potting: Repot every year in late spring, when not in flower. It likes a small pot with a bark and sphagnum mix. When it has grown large enough, the plant can be divided.

After flowering: When the flowers die, cut the stem back to about 1 in (3 cm). Continue the watering and feeding regime all year.

Paphiopedilum Ianthe Stage

This handsome Slipper orchid has marbled foliage and prefers warmer temperatures than the plain-foliaged varieties. It has interesting, hairy stems, and the flowers stay in good condition for around two months. It is a slow-growing plant.

INDOOR CARE

Temperature: The plant grows best in daytime temperatures above 70°F (21°C), with nights not below 60°F (16°C). Avoid placing too close to a radiator or in a draft.

Light: Partial shade is ideal.

Watering: Water thoroughly from the top and allow it to drain. Try to keep the growing medium moist, but not too wet. Take care that water does not lodge between the leaves or in the center.

> **TIP** If water does lodge between the leaves or in the center, just dab lightly with some twisted tissue to soak up the excess.

Humidity: The higher the temperature, the higher the humidity required.

Feeding: Include half-strength orchid fertilizer in three out of four waterings.

Potting: Repot every year in late spring, when not in flower. It likes a small pot with a bark and sphagnum mix. When it has grown large enough, the plant can be divided.

After flowering; When the flowers die, cut the stem back to about 1 in (3 cm). Continue the watering and feeding regime all year.

Paphiopedilum insigne

The plant usually produces a single, glossy flower on each stem in the fall or early winter. This is one of the cooler-growing varieties of Slipper orchid, which was very popular in Victorian times.

INDOOR CARE

Temperature: Plants grow best in daytime temperatures of 57–64°F (14–18°C), with nights not below 50°F (10°C). Avoid placing too close to a radiator or in a draft.

Light: Partial shade is ideal.

Watering: Water thoroughly from the top and allow it to drain. Try to keep the growing medium moist, but not too wet. Take care that water does not lodge between the leaves or in the center.

> **TIP** If water does lodge between the leaves or in the center, just dab lightly with some twisted tissue to soak up the excess.

Humidity: The higher the temperature, the higher the humidity required.

Feeding: Include half-strength orchid fertilizer in three out of four waterings.

Potting: Repot every year in late spring, when not in flower. It likes a small pot with a bark and sphagnum mix. When it has grown large enough, the plant can be divided.

After flowering: When the flowers die, cut the stem back to about 1 in (3 cm). Continue the watering and feeding regime all year.

Paphiopedilum Maudiae

This handsome Slipper orchid, with marbled foliage, is slow-growing. It produces a single flower on each stem. There are many similar Slipper orchids available, in colors ranging from apple green to deep wine red.

INDOOR CARE

Temperature: It prefers daytime temperatures of around 70°F (21°C), with nights not below 64°F (18°C). Avoid placing too close to a radiator or in a draft.

Light: Indirect sunlight is ideal. Shading will be needed in a conservatory.

Watering: Water thoroughly from the top and allow it to drain. Try to keep the growing medium moist, but not wet. Take care that water does not lodge between the leaves or in the center of the plant.

> **TIP** If water does lodge between the leaves or in the center, dab lightly with some twisted tissue to soak up the excess.

Humidity: The higher the temperature, the higher the humidity required.

Feeding: Include half-strength orchid fertilizer in three out of four waterings.

Potting: Repot every year in late spring, when not in flower. It likes a small pot and a bark and sphagnum mix.

After flowering: When the flowers die, cut the stem back to about 1 in (3 cm). Continue the watering and feeding regime all year.

Paphiopedilum niveum

This handsome and slow-growing orchid produces pretty, long-lasting white flowers during the winter. Each stem has one or two flowers that open in succession.

INDOOR CARE

Temperature: The plant prefers daytime temperatures above 70°F (21°C), with nights not below 64°F (18°C). Avoid placing too close to a radiator or in a draft.

Light: Indirect sunlight is ideal. Shading will be needed in a conservatory.

Watering: Water thoroughly from the top and allow it to drain. Try to keep the growing medium moist, but not wet. Take care that water does not lodge between the leaves or in the center of the plant.

> **TIP** If water does lodge between the leaves or in the center, dab lightly with some twisted tissue to soak up the excess.

Humidity: The higher the temperature, the higher the humidity required.

Feeding: Include half-strength orchid fertilizer in three out of four waterings.

Potting: Repot every year in late spring, when not in flower. It likes a small pot and a bark and sphagnum mix. When the plant is large enough, it can be divided.

After flowering: When the flowers die, cut the stem back to about 1 in (3 cm). Continue the watering and feeding regime all year.

Paphiopedilum Pinocchio

This orchid's perky flowers are a remarkable color combination of pale pinks and yellows, making it an unusual pot plant. It usually produces two or three flowers on each stem, which bloom in succession.

INDOOR CARE

Temperature: The plant prefers daytime temperatures above 70 °F (21°C), with nights not below 60°F (16°C). Avoid placing too close to a radiator or in a draft.

Light: Indirect sunlight is ideal. Shade will be needed in a conservatory.

Watering: Water thoroughly from the top when the growing medium is almost dry and allow it to drain. Try to keep the growing medium just moist, but not wet. Take care that water does not lodge between the leaves or in the center of the plant.

Humidity: The higher the temperature, the higher the humidity required.

TIP If water does lodge between the leaves or in the center of the plant, dab lightly with some twisted tissue to soak up the excess.

Feeding: Include half-strength orchid fertilizer in three out of four waterings.

Potting: Repot every year in late spring, when not in flower. It likes a small pot and a bark and sphagnum mix.

After flowering: When the flowers die, cut the stem back to about 1 in (3 cm). Continue the watering and feeding regime all year.

Paphiopedilum primulinum

This is another of the cooler-growing varieties of Slipper orchid. When the plant is small, it will usually produce two glossy flowers on each stem between winter and early spring.

INDOOR CARE

Temperature: It grows best in daytime temperatures of 57–64°F (14–18°C), with nights not below 50°F (10°C). Avoid placing too close to a radiator or in a draft.

Light: Prefers partial shade. Shade will be needed in a conservatory.

Watering: Water thoroughly from the top and allow it to drain. Try to keep the growing medium moist, but not wet. Take care that water does not lodge between the leaves or in the center of the plant.

> **TIP** If water does lodge between the leaves or in the center, dab lightly with some twisted tissue to soak up the excess.

Humidity: The higher the temperature, the higher the humidity required.

Feeding: Include half-strength orchid fertilizer in three out of four waterings.

Potting: Repot every year after flowering. It likes a small pot and a bark and sphagnum moss mix. When the plant is large enough, it can be divided.

After flowering: When the flowers die, cut the stem back to about 1 in (3 cm). Continue the watering and feeding regime all year.

Paphiopedilum Transvaal

This handsome slipper orchid, with marbled foliage, is a slow-growing houseplant. It usually produces two or more flowers per stem. The unusual "wings" are slightly twisted and have hairy margins.

INDOOR CARE

Temperature: It prefers daytime temperatures of 70–82°F (21–28°C), with nights not below 64°F (18°C). Avoid placing too close to a radiator or in a draft.

Light: Indirect sunlight is ideal. Shading will be needed in a conservatory.

Watering: Water thoroughly from the top and allow it to drain. Try to keep the growing medium moist, but not wet. Take care that water does not lodge between the leaves or in the center of the plant.

> **TIP** If water does lodge between the leaves or in the center, dab lightly with some twisted tissue to soak up the excess.

Humidity: The higher the temperature, the higher the humidity required.

Feeding: Include half-strength orchid fertilizer in three out of four waterings.

Potting: Repot every year in late spring, when not in flower. It likes a small pot and a bark and sphagnum moss mix.

After flowering: When the flowers die, cut the stem back to about 1 in (3 cm). Continue the watering and feeding regime all year.

Phaius tankervilleae

This is a tall, striking plant with large leaves, so choose a position carefully. In the wild, it can reach 6 ft (2 m) in height, but more commonly attains 2 ft (60 cm). The showy flowers have attractive tubular lips that point downward and the large leaves are handsomely pleated.

INDOOR CARE

Temperature: *Phaius tankervilleae* grows best in daytime temperatures above 65°F (18°C), with nights not below 55°F (13°C). Avoid placing too close to a radiator or in a draft.
Light: Good indirect light is ideal. Shading will be needed in a conservatory.

Watering: Water frequently when the plant is growing. Water thoroughly from the top when the growing medium is almost dry and allow it to drain. Take care not to splash water on the leaves. Water sparingly during its resting period, keeping the plant almost dry.
Humidity: It enjoys a humid atmosphere.
Feeding: Include orchid fertilizer in three out of four waterings.
Potting: Repot every three years in late spring, when not in flower. When the plant has grown sufficiently large, it can be divided.
After flowering: When the flowers die, cut the stem back to about 1 in (3 cm). Water less frequently—about every two weeks—but continue to feed. Resume frequent watering when new growth starts to appear.

Phalaenopsis amabilis

The moth orchid makes an ideal plant for a centrally heated home and has been used countless times in breeding. Its flowers may look delicate, but they are actually quite robust—often remaining in good condition for over three months. One stem can carry nine or more flowers and a plant may have more than one stem, depending on age. Flower spikes may appear any season, and this orchid usually reflowers within the year.

INDOOR CARE

Temperature: It grows best in daytime temperatures above 68°F (20°C), with nights not below 60°F (16°C). Avoid placing the plant too close to a radiator or in a draft.

Light: As it enjoys the dappled light of the forest in the wild, indirect sunlight is ideal.

Watering: Water thoroughly from the top when the growing medium is almost dry and allow it to drain. Take care that water does not lodge between the leaves, and keep the center of the plant dry. Moisture from the atmosphere is absorbed by the aerial roots outside the pot.

> **TIP** Should water become lodged between the leaves, dab lightly with some twisted tissue to soak up the excess.

Humidity: The higher the temperature, the higher the humidity required. If you live in a dry climate, stand the plant on a moist gravel tray to create a microclimate and assist growth. Make sure that the base of the pot is above the water level. Placing it on an upturned saucer helps to lift it slightly. Including ferns on the tray not only makes an attractive arrangement, but also improves humidity levels. Gently misting the plants early in the morning also helps.

Feeding: Include orchid fertilizer in three out of four waterings.

Potting: Repot every other year between March and June, but not when in flower.

After flowering: When the flowers die, cut the stem back to just above a node (*see diagram, page 40*), leaving around 8 in (20 cm) of stem. Often a secondary spike, or flower stem, is produced from this node.

> **TIP** If a large, healthy plant fails to produce a flower spike in a reasonable time (eight months), reduce the temperature by 10°F (5°C) for four weeks to encourage flowering.

Phalaenopsis Brother Little Amaglad

This orchid has small, but extremely long-lasting flowers. It may produce flower spikes any season and usually reflowers within the year. Plants typically have two stems. As a shorter variety, it is easier to position.

INDOOR CARE

Temperature: It grows best in daytime temperatures above 68°F (20°C), with nights not below 60°F (16°C). Avoid placing the plant too close to a radiator or in a draft.

Light: Indirect sunlight is ideal.

Watering: Water thoroughly from the top when the growing medium is almost dry and allow it to drain. Take care that water does not lodge between the leaves, and keep the center of the plant dry. Moisture is absorbed from the atmosphere by the aerial roots outside the pot.

> **TIP** Should water become lodged between the leaves, dab lightly with some twisted tissue to soak up the excess.

Humidity: The higher the temperature, the higher the humidity required. If you live in a dry atmosphere, stand the plant on a moist gravel tray to create a microclimate and assist growth. Make sure that the base of the pot is above the water level. Placing it on an upturned saucer will help to lift it slightly. Including ferns on the tray not only makes an attractive arrangement, but also improves humidity levels. Gently misting the plants early in the morning also helps.

Feeding: Include orchid fertilizer in three out of four waterings.

Potting: This should usually be carried out every other year in late spring, but not when in flower.

After flowering: When the flowers die, cut the stem back, just below where the lowest flower was produced. A secondary spike or flower stem may grow from the highest node (*see diagram, page 40*), If the stem turns brown, cut it back to about 1 in (3 cm). After several months, new stems will grow from the base of the plant.

> **TIP** If a large, healthy plant fails to produce a flower spike in a reasonable time (eight months), reduce the temperature by 10°F (5°C) for four weeks to encourage flowering.

Phalaenopsis Brother Sara Gold

This is a modern example of why the moth orchid has become such a popular houseplant. Its flowers often remain in good condition for over three months. It may produce flower spikes in any season and usually reflowers within the year. Plants typically have two stems.

Other moth orchids to consider: hundreds of hybrids are registered every year. They come in many colors, plain and patterned, and in a wide range of flower sizes.

INDOOR CARE

Temperature: The plant grows best in daytime temperatures above 68°F (20°C), with nights not below 60°F (16°C). Avoid placing the plant too close to a radiator or in a draft.
Light: Indirect sunlight is ideal.
Watering: Water thoroughly from the top when the growing medium is almost dry and allow it to drain. Take care that water does not lodge between the leaves, and keep the center of the plant dry. Moisture is absorbed from the atmosphere by the aerial roots outside the pot.
Humidity: The higher the temperature, the higher the humidity required. If you live in a dry climate, standing the plant on a moist gravel tray will create a microclimate and assist growth. Make sure that the base of the pot is above the water level. Putting the pot on an upturned saucer will help to lift it slightly. Including some ferns on the tray would not only make an attractive arrangement, but also improve humidity levels. Gently misting the plants early in the morning also helps.

> **TIP** Should water become lodged between the leaves, dab lightly with some twisted tissue to soak up the excess.

Feeding: Include orchid fertilizer in three out of four waterings.
Potting: This should usually be carried out every other year in late spring, but not when in flower.
After flowering: When the flowers die, cut the stem back to just above a node (*see diagram, page 40*), leaving around 8 in (20 cm) of stem. Often a secondary spike, or flower stem, is produced from this node.

> **TIP** If a large, healthy plant fails to produce a flower spike in a reasonable time (eight months), reduce the temperature by 10°F (5°C) for four weeks to encourage flowering.

Above: *Phalaenopsis* Dragon's Charm. For care instructions,
see the profile opposite, but note that Dragon's Charm has
no fragrance.

Above: *Phalaenopsis* Happy Kathleen. For care instructions, see the profile on page 124, but note that Happy Kathleen has no fragrance.

Above: *Phalaenopsis* Taisuco Snow. For care instructions, see the profile on page 124, but note that Taisuco Snow has no fragrance.

Phalaenopsis violacea

This moth orchid is strikingly different from the usual pot plant, *Phalaenopsis*, having large leaves and short stems. It produces two or three highly fragrant, long-lasting flowers, usually in late summer.

INDOOR CARE

Temperature: It grows best in daytime temperatures above 68°F (20°C), with nights not below 60°F (16°C). Avoid placing the plant too close to a radiator or in a draft.
Light: Indirect sunlight is ideal.
Watering: Water thoroughly from the top when the growing medium is almost dry and allow it to drain. Take care that water does not lodge between the leaves, and keep the center of the plant dry. Moisture is absorbed from the atmosphere by the aerial roots outside the pot.

> **TIP** If water does lodge between the leaves, dab lightly with some twisted tissue to soak up the excess.

Humidity: The higher the temperature, the higher the humidity required. Gently mist the plants early in the morning if the air is dry and temperatures are above 71°F (22°C). Placing it on a humidity tray would also be beneficial.
Feeding: Include orchid fertilizer in three out of four waterings.
Potting: Repot every other year, but not when in flower.
After flowering: When the flowers die, cut the stem back to 1 in (3 cm) from the base. Continue to water and feed.

Phalaenopsis Zuma's Pixie

This hybrid is bred from the species *equestris* to produce plants that have many small, long-lasting-flowers. It can bloom during any season, and usually reflowers within the year. Plants typically have two or more stems.

Other moth orchids from this line of breeding to consider: Be Tris and Brother Pico Pink.

INDOOR CARE

Temperature: It grows best in daytime temperatures above 68°F (20°C), with nights not below 60°F (16°C). Avoid placing too close to a radiator or in a draft.

Light: Good, indirect sunlight is ideal.

Watering: It is happy to be kept a little drier than most moth orchids. Water thoroughly from the top when the growing medium is just dry and allow it to drain. Take care that water does not lodge between the leaves, and keep the center of the plant dry. Some moisture is also absorbed from the atmosphere by the aerial roots outside the pot.

Humidity: The higher the temperature, the higher the humidity required. If you live in a dry climate, stand the plant on a moist gravel tray to create a microclimate and assist growth. Make sure that the base of the pot is above the water level. Placing it on an upturned saucer will lift it slightly. Including ferns on the tray not only makes an attractive arrangement, but also helps humidity levels. Gently misting the plants early in the morning also helps.

> **TIP** If water does lodge between the leaves, dab lightly with some twisted tissue to soak up the excess.

Feeding: Include orchid fertilizer in three out of four waterings.

Potting: Repot every other year in late spring, but not when in flower.

After flowering: When the flowers die, cut the stem back to 1 in (3 cm) from the base. Continue to water and feed.

Phragmipedium besseae

This is one of the most recent discoveries of the orchid world. It was found in 1981 in South America. These dramatic-looking plants produce up to four spectacular blooms on separate stems. Most are vivid red or orange in color. The flowers open in succession and, unusually, do not appear to wilt. When their time is over, they fall off the plant, in seemingly perfect condition.

Other *Phragmipedium* can be found in a range of colors, from soft pink to green.

INDOOR CARE

Temperature: It grows best in daytime temperatures of around 68°F (20°C), with cooler nights not below 55°F (13°C). It likes an airy spot, but avoid placing too close to a radiator or in a draft.

Light: Light from a west-facing window is ideal.

Watering: It likes plenty of water when growing. Water thoroughly from the top when the surface of the growing medium is nearly dry and allow it to drain. Never let it sit in water.

Humidity: The higher the temperature, the higher the humidity required. If you live in a dry climate, stand the plant on a moist gravel tray to create a microclimate and assist growth.

Feeding: Include half-strength orchid fertilizer in three out of four waterings.

Potting: This should usually be carried out every other year in spring, but not when in flower. It prefers to grow in large clumps, rather than be divided frequently.

After flowering: When the flowers die or the stem becomes too tall and ungainly, cut the stem back to 1 in (3 cm) from the base. Continue to water and feed all year.

Phragmipedium pearcei

This orchid family is often mistaken for *Paphiopedilum* as the flowers have a similar pouched lip. The blooms have pretty, twisted petals and are carried on stiff stems. The slender, dark green leaves arch attractively. The flowers open in succession on this compact plant, each flower lasting for a couple of weeks. Unusually, the blooms do not appear to wilt. When their time is over, they fall off the plant in seemingly perfect condition. This orchid can be found in flower at most times of the year.

INDOOR CARE

Temperature: It grows best in daytime temperatures of about 68°F (20°C), with cooler nights not below 55°F (13°C). It likes an airy spot, but avoid placing too close to a radiator or in a draft.

Light: Light from a west-facing window is ideal.

Watering: It likes plenty of water when growing. Water thoroughly from the top when the surface of the growing medium is nearly dry and allow it to drain. Never let it sit in water.

Humidity: The higher the temperature, the higher the humidity required. If you live in a dry climate, standing the plant on a moist gravel tray will create a microclimate and assist growth.

Feeding: Include half-strength orchid fertilizer in three out of four waterings.

Potting: This should usually be carried out every other year in spring, but not when in flower. It prefers to grow in large clumps, rather than be divided frequently.

After flowering: When the flowers die, cut the stem back to 1 in (3 cm) from the base. Continue to water and feed all year.

Pleione formosana 'Blush of Dawn'

Commonly known as the Indian Crocus, this plant produces one or two flowers with a pretty fringed lip from each pseudobulb during the spring. After vigorous growth, it loses its leaves over winter.

Other *Pleione* to consider: there are many available, mainly in shades of pink or white.

INDOOR CARE

Temperature: The plant grows best in cooler temperatures. It has a definite annual cycle, enjoying warm summers and cool winters. It will struggle with daytime temperatures above 77°F (25°C). Prefers frost-free winter nights of 50°F (10°C) or even cooler.

TIP If you live in a region where the winters are warmer than this, a spell in the refrigerator could be helpful.

Light: It requires good, indirect light. A north-facing window is ideal.

Watering: Water freely while the leaves and roots are growing. Water sparingly while in flower, keeping the growing medium just damp. Reduce watering as the leaves yellow, and stop completely when the leaves become brown and drop off.

Feeding: Regular feeding of a balanced fertilizer is beneficial while the plant is growing.

Potting: Repot every year when dormant. It likes a small pot and a free-draining growing medium of sphagnum moss, fine bark and perlite. Approximately one-third of the bulb should be above the surface of the growing medium level. Space about 1 in (3 cm) apart.

After flowering: Allow a cool rest period of a few months during the winter.

Rossioglossum grande

Commonly known as the Clown orchid, the plant produces multi-flowered spikes with dramatic blooms between late fall and early winter. Each bright yellow and brick-red flower is about 5 in (13 cm) wide and has a waxy texture. They open in succession, each lasting around two weeks, giving a stunning show for over two months.

INDOOR CARE

Temperature: It prefers daytime temperatures of around 61–64 °F (16–18°C), with nights not below 55°F (13°C). However, it can tolerate higher temperatures for a short time, as long as humidity and air movement are increased. Avoid placing it too close to a radiator or in a draft.

Light: It needs protection from full, midday sun. Plants can be grown in an east- or west-facing window.

Watering: Water the growing medium thoroughly from the top and allow it to drain. Never let the growing medium dry out completely while growing.

Humidity: Most homes will be suitable, but if you live in a dry climate, stand the plant on a moist gravel tray to help increase humidity.

Feeding: Include half-strength orchid fertilizer in three out of four waterings.

Potting: Repot every other year in the spring. Use a medium-grade orchid growing mix or bark.

After flowering: When the blooms die, cut the flower stem back to about 1 in (3 cm). Continue watering and feeding, but reduce the frequency in the fall and winter and allow the growing medium to dry out completely between waterings.

Vuylstekeara Cambria

This proven pot plant produces spikes of attractive and long-lasting flowers that often remain in good condition for over two months. Plants have one or more stems, depending on age. One of the most famous varieties is 'Plush.'

Other *Vuylstekeara* to consider: Edna Stamperland, Linda Isler, Manhattan Red.

INDOOR CARE

Temperature: The plant grows best in daytime temperatures above 66°F (19°C), with nights not below 55°F (13°C). Although reasonably tolerant, it will struggle with temperatures above 77°F (25°C). Avoid placing it too close to a radiator or in a draft.

Light: An east- or west-facing window is ideal.

Watering: Water the growing medium thoroughly from the top and allow it to drain. Never let it dry out completely. Take care that water does not lodge between the leaves and the pseudobulbs.

> **TIP** If water does lodge between the leaves and the pseudobulbs, dab lightly with some twisted tissue to soak up the excess.

Humidity: The higher the temperature, the higher the humidity required. If you live in a dry climate, stand the plant on a moist gravel tray to create a microclimate and assist growth.

Feeding: Include half-strength orchid fertilizer in three out of four waterings.

Potting: Repot every other year in the early fall, but not when in flower.

After flowering: When the flowers die, cut back the stems to about 1 in (3 cm). Continue watering and feeding, but reduce the frequency of watering as temperatures start to drop.

Wilsonara Marvida

Suitable for a centrally heated home, this orchid is more tolerant than its relative, the *Odontoglossum*. Its flowers often remain in good condition for over two months. Aerial roots can sometimes be seen outside the pot.

Other *Wilsonara* to consider: Tiger Brew, Ash Trees, Franz Wichmann, Lisa Devos, Stirling Tiger, Zoe's Fire.

INDOOR CARE

Temperature: It grows best in daytime temperatures of around 68°F (20°C), with nights not below 55°F (13°C). Although reasonably tolerant, it will struggle with temperatures above 77°F (25°C). Avoid placing too close to a radiator or in a draft.

Light: An east- or west-facing window is ideal.

Watering: Water the growing medium thoroughly from the top when it is almost dry and allow it to drain. Never let it dry out completely.

Humidity: The higher the temperature, the higher the humidity required. If you live in a dry climate, stand the plant on a moist gravel tray to create a microclimate and assist growth.

Feeding: Include half-strength orchid fertilizer in three out of four waterings.

Potting: This should usually be done every other year. Repot when you can see 2–3 in (5–8 cm) of new growth.

After flowering: When the flowers die, cut back the stems to about 1 in (3 cm). Continue watering and feeding, but reduce the frequency of watering as temperatures start to cool.

Zygoneria Adelaide Meadows

When mature, this plant will produce several spikes of fragrant flowers. Peak flowering time is usually early spring, and it can rebloom within the year. This particular hybrid comes in apple greens and various shades of purple and brown. Patterning will vary from plant to plant, as they are seed-raised.

> **TIP** Although the vast majority of this orchid family are fragrant, a few are not. To avoid disappointment, check this before you buy.

Other *Zygoneria* to consider: Adelaide Charmer, Dynamite, Elder Park, Adelaide Oval, Adelaide Parklands, Kuitpo.

INDOOR CARE

Temperature: *Zygoneria* Adelaide Meadows grows best in daytime temperatures of about 68°F (20°C), with nights not below 55°F (13°C). However, for short periods it can tolerate temperatures as high as 95°F (35°C), as well as much lower temperatures.

Light: It prefers light from an east- or west-facing window.

Watering: Never let your plant completely dry out. Water the growing medium thoroughly from the top and allow it to drain. This is best done in the morning so that the foliage will have time to dry before temperatures drop.

Humidity: It prefers an atmosphere that isn't too dry. The higher the temperature, the higher the humidity required. If you live in a dry climate, stand the plant on a moist gravel tray to create a microclimate and assist growth.

> **TIP** Good air movement will help dry the leaves after watering. If the foliage remains damp, there is a risk of crown rot at the base of the leaves.

Feeding: Include orchid fertilizer in three out of four waterings.

Potting: Repot this vigorous grower every spring or early summer. Choose a container with just enough space for only two new pseudobulbs to develop before next repotting. Use a well-aerated, free-draining orchid mix.

After flowering: When the flowers die, cut back the stems to about 1 in (3 cm). Continue watering and feeding, but reduce the frequency of watering as temperatures drop.

> **TIP** If a strong healthy plant with a new pseudobulb is reluctant to flower, try placing it in a cooler room for a couple of weeks when new growth is beginning to emerge.

Zygopetalum Blue Lake

A vigorous grower and very tolerant, this plant is ideal for a novice grower. When mature, it will produce many spikes of fragrant flowers, each bloom lasting around two weeks. Peak flowering time is late winter to early spring and it sometimes reblooms in the summer.

> **TIP** Although the vast majority of this orchid family are fragrant, a few are not. To avoid disappointment, check this before you buy.

Other *Zygopetalum* to consider: B G White, Big Country, Centenary, Granite Island, Myponga, Nairne.

INDOOR CARE

Temperature: The plant grows best in daytime temperatures of about 68°F (20°C), with nights not below 55°F (13°C). However, for short periods it can tolerate temperatures as high as 95°F (35°C), as well as much lower temperatures. *Zygopetalum* can survive brief spells with night temperatures of just above freezing, provided that daytime temperatures are warmer.

Light: It prefers light from an east- or west-facing window is ideal.

Watering: Never let your plant completely dry out. Water the growing medium

thoroughly from the top and allow it to drain. This is best done in the morning so that the foliage will have time to dry before temperatures drop.

> **TIP** Good air movement will help dry the leaves after watering. If the foliage remains damp, there is a risk of crown rot at the base of the leaves.

Humidity: It prefers a comfortable, but not dry atmosphere. The higher the temperature, the higher the humidity required. If you live in a dry climate, stand the plant on a moist gravel tray to create a microclimate and assist growth.

Feeding: Include orchid fertilizer in three out of four waterings.

Potting: Repot every spring or early summer. Choose a container with just enough space for only two new pseudobulbs to develop before next repotting. Use a well-aerated, free-draining orchid mix.

After flowering: When the flowers die, cut back the stems to about 1 in (3 cm). Continue watering and feeding, but reduce the frequency of watering as temperatures drop.

> **TIP** If a strong healthy plant with a new pseudobulb is reluctant to flower, try placing it in a cooler room for a couple of weeks when new growth is beginning to emerge.

Zygopetalum Port Vincent

The unusual color combinations of purple, greens and browns, together with its scent, give this orchid great appeal. When mature, the plant will produce several spikes of fragrant flowers. Peak flowering time is usually late winter to early spring. Each flower lasts around two weeks. Patterning will vary from plant to plant as they are seed raised. Other *Zygopetalum* to consider: B G White, Big Country, Centenary, Granite Island, Myponga, Nairne.

> **TIP** Although the vast majority of this orchid family are fragrant, a few are not. To avoid disappointment, check this before you buy.

INDOOR CARE

Temperature: It grows best in daytime temperatures of around 68°F (20°C), with nights not below 55°F (13°C). However, for short periods it can tolerate temperatures as high as 95°F (35°C), as well as much lower temperatures. *Zygopetalum* can survive brief spells with night temperatures of just above freezing, provided that daytime temperatures are warmer.

> **TIP** Good air movement will help dry the leaves after watering. If the foliage remains damp, there is a risk of crown rot at the base of the leaves.

Light: It prefers light from an east- or west-facing window.

Watering: Never let your plant completely dry out. Water the growing medium thoroughly from the top and allow it to drain. This is best done in the morning so that the foliage will have time to dry before temperatures drop.

Humidity: It prefers an atmosphere that isn't too dry. The higher the temperature, the more humidity is required. If you live in a dry climate, stand the plant on a moist gravel tray to create a microclimate and assist growth.

Feeding: Include orchid fertilizer in three out of four waterings.

Potting: Repot every spring or early summer. Choose a container with just enough space for only two new pseudobulbs to develop before next repotting. Use a well-aerated, free-draining orchid mix.

After flowering: When the flowers die, cut back the stems to about 1 in (3 cm). Continue watering and feeding, but reduce the frequency of watering as temperatures start to drop.

Index

Useful addresses

American Orchid Society
16700 AOS Lane
Delray Beach
Florida
33446-4351
Tel: +1 (0)561-404-2000
Fax: +1 (0)561-404-2100
Email:TheAOS@aos.org
www.orchidweb.org

CITES/Plant health
USDA Permit Services
Tel: 1-877-770-5990
www.orchidweb.org/permits.html

U.K.
McBean's Orchids
Cooksbridge, Lewes
East Sussex
BN8 4PR
Tel: 01273 400228
Fax: 01273 401181
Email: sales@mcbeansorchids.co.uk
www.mcbeansorchids.co.uk

British Orchid Council
www.go.to/british-orchid-council

British Orchid Growers Association
Hon. Sec. Mrs J Plested
38 Florence Road
College Town
Sandhurst
Berkshire
GU47 0QD
Tel/Fax: 01276 32947

www.boga.org.uk
Hardy Orchid Society
www.hardyorchidsociety.org.uk

Orchid Society of Great Britain
www.orchid-society-gb.org.uk

The Scottish Orchid Society
Secretary, Alan Benson
Email: secretary@scottishorchids.info

DEFRA
CITES: Import/export certification
Global Wildlife Division
1-17 Temple Quay House
2 The Square
Temple Quay
Bristol
BS1 6EB
Tel: 0117 372 8749
Fax: 0117 372 8206
Email: wildlife.licensing@defra.gsi.gov.uk
www.ukcites.gov.uk

PLANT HEALTH: Phytosanitary inspection
Defra, Plant Health Services Delivery Unit
Room 334, Foss House
Kings Pool
York
YO1 7PX

Plant Health HQT
Tel: 01904 455174
Fax: 01904 455197
Area contact list can be found on:-
www.defra.gov.uk/planth/senior.htm

Acknowledgments

Chrysalis Books Group Plc is committed to respecting the intellectual property rights of others. We have therefore taken all reasonable efforts to ensure that the reproduction of all content on these pages is done with the full consent of copyright owners. If you are aware of any unintentional omissions please
contact the company directly so that any necessary corrections may be made for future editions.

B= Bottom; T= Top; R= Right; C= Center; L= Left.

4 ©Liz Johnson; 5 ©Liz Johnson; 7 ©Liz Johnson; 8–9 Chrysalis Image Library/©Helen Ku; 10 ©Liz Johnson; 11B Chrysalis Image Library; 13T Chrysalis Image Library; 13BR Chrysalis Image Library; 16–17 Chrysalis Image Library; 19T Chrysalis Image Library; 19B Chrysalis Image Library; 20 Chrysalis Image Library; 20R Chrysalis Image Library; 20B Chrysalis Image Library; 24 Chrysalis Image Library; 25C Chrysalis Image Library; 25B Chrysalis Image Library; 26C Chrysalis Image Library; 26B ©Chris Martin Bahr/Rex Features; 27 ©Chris Martin Bahr/Rex Features; 28–29 Chrysalis Image Library; 32 Chrysalis Image Library; 33L Chrysalis Image Library; 33B Chrysalis Image Library; 34 Chrysalis Image Library; 35 ©Liz Johnson; 38–39 Chrysalis Image Library; 40T Chrysalis Image Library; 40B Chrysalis Image Library; 41 ©Liz Johnson; 49 ©Liz Johnson;50 ©Liz Johnson; 51 ©Johan Hermans; 52 ©Liz Johnson; 53 ©Eric Crichton Photos; 55 ©McBean's Picture Library; 57 ©Garden World Images; 58 ©McBean's Picture Library; 72 ©Jerry Harpur; 78 ©Felicity Cole; 80 ©Eric Crichton Photos; 82 ©Eric Crichton Photos; 86 ©Johan Hermans; 89 ©Eric Crichton Photos; 93 ©Eric Crichton Photos; 95TR ©Liz Johnson; 98 ©McBean's Picture Library; 102 ©Liz Johnson; 103 ©Brian Carter/Garden Picture Library; 110 ©McBean's Picture Library; 111 © Eric Crichton Photos; 113 ©Eric Crichton Photos; 116 ©McBean's Picture Library; 128 ©Eric Crichton Photos; 129 ©Eric Crichton Photos; 130 ©McBean's Picture Library.

All other photographs taken by Neil Sutherland.

With thanks to Sally Cole for her help.